FINDING
MEANING

A QUEST FOR TRUTH

William Blakeslee Chapel, PhD

Copyright © 2022 William Blakeslee Chapel, PhD.

All rights reserved. No part of this book may be reproduced, stored, or transmitted by any means—whether auditory, graphic, mechanical, or electronic—without written permission of both publisher and author, except in the case of brief excerpts used in critical articles and reviews. Unauthorized reproduction of any part of this work is illegal and is punishable by law.

The narrative portion of this book is based on real times, places, events, and persons. While depicting real persons, their names are fictitious and do not represent persons living or dead with like or similar names, the exception being those persons who are readily recognized because of their notoriety; they are referred to by their actual names. Scripture references in the doctrinal portions are the Word of God, while interpretation expresses the belief of the author.

Scripture taken from the New American Standard Bible, Copyright © 1960, 1962, 1963, 1968, 1971, 1972, 1973, 1975, 1977, 1995 by the Lockman Foundation. Used by permission.

ISBN: 979-8-88640-016-8 (sc)
ISBN: 979-8-88640-017-5 (hc)
ISBN: 979-8-88640-018-2 (e)

Because of the dynamic nature of the Internet, any web addresses or links contained in this book may have changed since publication and may no longer be valid. The views expressed in this work are solely those of the author and do not necessarily reflect the views of the publisher, and the publisher hereby disclaims any responsibility for them.

One Galleria Blvd., Suite 1900, Metairie, LA 70001
1-888-421-2397

CHAPTER 1

Humankind has fallen far from the ideal that God created in our first ancestors, Adam and Eve. As we approach the last days of this present age, we witness ever increasing brutality and disregard for one another. Yet, we are all heavenly creatures, destined for eternal life. Think about that for a moment. This truth, if truly internalized, is exciting beyond words. Finding true and lasting hope is based on the depth and breadth of God's love. The following is one person's quest for Truth, and was found in the meaning of life.

The times in Detroit were cold and dreary during the winter of 1934; December was in the throes of an unusually snowy, cold spell in tandem with the continuing drag of the Great Depression. These factors made almost everyone depressed and vulnerable to one extent or another.

But the winds of change were sweeping through the landscape. Henry Ford was changing the cultural and social climate in the city and country as very few other persons were at the time, an exception being his close camping friend, Thomas Edison. The two of them, along with Harvey Firestone and the naturalist John Burroughs, would motor north in their Cadillac and Pierce Arrow touring cars, followed by a Ford truck specially outfitted as a traveling kitchen. Henry Ford liked to tell the wistful yarn about the time the caravan stopped at a service station to replace a headlight on one of the vehicles. As the story goes, Ford said to the attendant, "By the way, you might be interested to hear that the man who invented the lamp is sitting out there in my car."

"You don't mean Thomas Edison?" the man gasped.

"Yes, and incidentally, my name is Henry Ford." Noting the brand of tire in the service station's racks, Ford added, "And one of the other men in the car makes those tires—Harvey Firestone."

The attendant's jaw dropped. Then he saw John Burroughs with his flowing beard, and his voice became skeptical: "Look here, mister, if you tell me that the old fellow with the whiskers out there is Santa Claus, I'm going to call the sheriff" (Collier, P. and Horowitz, D. (1987, p.91). *The Fords: An American Epic*. New York: Summit Books).

The four of them would meet and discuss the world's problems and many mundane issues as well at Ford's retreat just north of the village of L'Anse in Michigan's beautiful Upper Peninsula. L'Anse is at the gateway to the Keweenaw Peninsula, a spectacular finger of land jutting out into Lake Superior, the giant freshwater inland sea. This is the lake of many moods, from tranquil in the summer months to violent in November. Many ships loaded with ore from the ports of Minnesota and Wisconsin found their depths as storms carried crews to their final resting place during the gales of November. When absent from the tranquil summer waves off Keweenaw Bay and the fragrant wood forests of the Huron Mountains that stretch out between the towns of Herman and Marquette, Ford's interests were in Dearborn, Michigan where he was developing a vertical manufacturing strategy. This integrative process included wood for the side panels of the wonderful "Woody" station wagon models harvested from the Ford forestry operations at Alberta, just a few miles southeast of L'Anse; rubber from Latin American plantations; other components from his plant in Iron River, also located in the Upper Peninsula; along with many other places and parts.

This was long before the next social and economic revolution, dubbed the Information Age, came on the world. This transformation brought billionaire neo-changelings to the Silicon Valley as the innovators of a virtual society. Ford built an automobile for the masses to enjoy; many decades later the computer changed society as no other mode of communication had since the invention of the printing press. First came primitive human-computer natural language dyads such as word processing and hypertext. Today's technological world is taking a turn down a slippery sliding slope toward the demise of privacy. Social networking wizards are changing lives with computer connectivity now utilized by various social medium networks, such as *Facebook (*recently renamed *Meta) and its* family of apps; alone having more than 3 billion subscribers routinely communicating with each other around the world. While the social media provide countless communication interchange opportunities, these social networking channels are at the same time bringing about a controlling and less private realm.

At least this is what's behind *Singularity*; that science researching and developing computational power with the goal of producing mind-like artificial intelligent decisions. In precursors to actual AI mental representations, we encounter social thought engineering. For example, one TicToc app user proposed that all logged on should slap a teacher; from this, at least one teacher was severely injured. We encounter many examples of *Singularity* in present day networking phenomena, captivating multi-millions in the world with the notion that life's decisions ought to be based on social group interaction rather than God designed communication. Misinformation relating to pandemic vaccinations is one example of 'groupthink' that is currently rampant on the social media.

With computing getting faster and faster, there may come a moment in time when artificial intelligence (AI) develops far beyond current capabilities to compete with human consciousness, to make ethical decisions. The backers of this strong AI concept believe it is only a matter of time until the powers of computers become equal to the intelligence of human minds. We see the primitive examples of singularity in the current social networking systems. Raymond Kurzwell is one of the advocates of the role of technology in our future, published his thoughts in the bestselling book *The Singularity Is Near: When Humans Transcend Biology* (2005). How this all affects truth and the future of planet Earth will be revisited later in this story, but now back to our narrative.

The Great Depression years from the Wall Street crash of 1929 when men of swagger lost fortunes overnight to the latter 1930s with all the ramifications of hopelessness, would give way to more hopeful times; If only the people could weather the current economic storms. A good part of the weathering took place in Detroit at the junction of Michigan Avenue and Trumbull, where the great green grass and excitement of Briggs Stadium and the Detroit Tigers already brought a reprieve to many.

Earlier in the century came Ty Cobb, the Georgia Peach, and Harry Heilmann, whose mellow voice brought a message of hope. After Heilmann's years as a stellar Tiger outfielder, the Hall of Famer announced the Tiger games on radio. More recent legions—Charlie Gehringer, "Hammerin'" Hank Greenberg, and all the other great boys of summer before, during, and after the economic demise of the thirties—helped bring about the reversal from despondency to relative hopefulness.

This didn't do much, however, to provide hope for the hurt and struggling homeless inhabitants on Michigan Avenue; at that time Detroit's skid row. Washington Boulevard, on the other hand, was an impressionistic portrait of the well-to-do (and those attempting to appear like the well-to-do; the top-hat-with-no-stockings set!) strolling from the Book Cadillac Hotel at one end to the Statler Hotel at the other. Between these two magnificent hostelry icons was a scene of those able to survive the economic woes since the financial crash of 1929: Gentry strolling down the avenue after reality-numbing three-martini lunches at the watering holes along the Boulevard back to their offices in the Penobscot Building and other high rises lining Griswold Street—the Motor City's small version of Wall Street—to sell their wares of bonds and stocks.

But looking westward, past Washington Boulevard, one saw an entirely different portrait of society: Men panhandled passersby to procure a jug of cheap wine to blunt the reality of their hopelessness. Crouched or lying on the street in gutters or in somewhat protected storefronts were the lost, the failed, the defeated—those men of broken dreams. Once, each one was young, innocent, and his mother's darling. What was it that happened along the way of life that sank these souls to such despair? Nightfall found them dead or, for the more fortunate, huddled in the shelter of love at the Detroit Rescue Mission or the Salvation Army residence, there to hear the old, old story of Jesus as the Savior to mankind. Some, after hearing the preacher expound on the Good News, were drawn by Holy Spirit to accept the gift of salvation and were born again to new spiritual life. Others heard but did not listen and returned to the highway of despair.

The more fortunate persons of the community usually avoided walking down Skid Row by riding the electric DSR streetcar or a Checker cab out Michigan Avenue on the way to watch the Tigers, as Spike Briggs' boys of summer played to hopefully reach the World Series. On balmy Sunday afternoons one could see families picnicking or sweethearts canoeing the waterways of Belle Isle. On one such day, the Great Houdini performed his escape artistry by diving off the Belle Isle Bridge into the Detroit River, his body heavily laden with chains and padlocks, only to soon "miraculously" emerge free from the metal encumbrances to accept loud applause from amazed parents and delighted children.

But for those cruising out Michigan Avenue, it was impossible not to at least glance to the right, out protected windows, at those much less able to survive the bleakness of reality. There was no Houdini trickery for escaping the chains of despair the men on the Row were shackled to; only their Creator held the key to a breakout from such encumbrances.

The automobile assembly lines spewing out the black and more recently colored machines (earlier, Mr. Ford would say a buyer could have any color desired as long as it was black) from his factories in Detroit, Highland Park, and the giant Rouge plant in Dearborn. Henry Ford created an additional production icon…one of compassion: the Henry Ford Hospital and Clinic. Struggles went on in that health care assembly line with 24/7 battles between life and death. One department, however, experienced more life than death along with daily doses of joy. Obstetric physicians and nurses delivered God's creatures as they emerged from comfort and security of the womb to face an unknown daunting world.

CHAPTER 2

This quest for Truth narrative begins with a December birthing at the Henry Ford Hospital that was traumatic and dangerous for mother and child. Both survived to return on Christmas Day to the family bungalow on St. Mary Street in northwest Detroit to celebrate with family and friends. This new citizen of the Motor City, is one Earnest B. de Beaubien. 'Ernie' as family and friends called him, would soon be captivated—no, driven—to find the answer to one question: What, if anything, is the meaning of life? Postmodern proponents theorize that there are countless pathways of truth to follow; take your pick—one is as good as another. However, Ernie was starting on his journey on the quest to find true, lasting Truth.

The hospital homecoming celebration that cold December of 1934 included, among others, the niece of Henry and Clara Bryant Ford. It was Clara's brother, Will Bryant, who offered Henry Ford $40 to help open a tool shop that ultimately led to the inventor's first primitive horseless carriage. Also present were Ernie's older sister, Norma, five years his senior and an important influence in the boy's life; his mother and father; and assorted other friends and relatives.

Ernie came into the world in the rough and tumble glory days of automobile pioneering in Detroit. There were, in addition to Ford, other industrial giants: Walter Chrysler, James Couzens, the Dodge brothers, as well as Billy Durant and the many faceless functionaries of the evolving General Motors conglomerate of Detroit, Flint, and Lansing. The city was quiet and elegant prior to the rapid growth and industrial sprawl brought on by America's love of the automobile. Major tree-lined thoroughfares spread out from the Detroit River like bicycle spokes from east to west. The beautiful Grand Boulevard transported motor and horse drawn passengers from elegant homes and apartments along East Jefferson Avenue and the Indian Village on the Detroit River on over to the west side of town.

Grand Boulevard crossed Woodward Avenue, the major traffic artery heading northward to the newly minted villages to be known as the suburbs. The grandest of these new suburbs were Birmingham, formerly known as Piety Hill for its many churches, and the even more exclusive Bloomfield Hills. These oases from the blunt reality of the 1930s housed many business and financial leaders who commuted to downtown Detroit every workday on the Grand Trunk Railroad. There were, according to the pundits of the commuter set: the *workers* (taking the 7:00 a.m. train), the *clerkers* (riding the 7:30 a.m. train), and the *shirkers* (aboard the 8:00 a.m. train). Stops along the way picked up clerks and management up-and-comers in Royal Oak, Ferndale, and Highland Park. However, many of the elite of the automobile makers, gravitated to the east side from Indian Village, where Henry's son, Edsel, once resided, out East Jefferson Avenue to the Grosse Pointe suburbs; each village becoming more affluent when traveling from Grosse Pointe Park to Grosse Pointe Farms. The first Henry Ford, however, preferred the cloistered country setting of Fairlane, his rural Dearborn fortress, avoiding the social scions of the east side. His son and later his grandchildren, however, preferred the upscale ease side enclaves.

Time, along with the FDR New Deal initiatives, healed much of the bleakness of the Great Depression. The thirties went by, along with many of the soup kitchen lines. Ernie was protected from the great depression in most ways, as his father was a successful Griswold Street investment banker. Homes were selling at rock-bottom prices and Ernie's family bought into the opportunity, purchasing a fine home in Birmingham for pennies on the pre-depression-based dollar.

After a few sandbox memories with neighborhood toddler chums in Detroit, Ernie started taking in the sights and visions of life in his world after moving to the new home in the suburbs. Friends cropped up like mushrooms, including the first friend he met, who lived next door. Antonio "Tony" Row was a good friend, and with Tony and his other friends and family, things for the four-year-old could not have been better. Except for a few skirmishes with the town bullies on walks to school or town, the boy was sheltered from the hardships and fears of the world that lingered only a few miles away southward down Woodward Avenue.

A few years later Ernie and Tony would hop on the Woodward Avenue electric streetcar and head downtown, then walk the few blocks out Michigan Avenue to the corner of Trumbull to watch two of their favorite players: Hoot Evers catching opposing teams' fly balls while patrolling left field, and Hal Newhouser sharing the competitive pitching mound limelight with Bob Feller of the Cleveland Indians.

Germany and Japan put an end, once and for all, to the bleak financial depression. Japan's attack of the U.S. Naval base at Pearl Harbor put Detroit, with its auto factories and skilled machine-shop workers, into high gear. The sprawling Ypsilanti Willow Run assembly plant was converted from making cars to bombers in support of the country's war mission against the Axis powers: Hitler, Mussolini, and the Emperor of Japan along with Tojo, his chief henchman. The heroes of the battlefields—land, air, and sea—joined with the behind-the-scene men and women of America in shepherding their gas and food ration stamps and the purchasing of war bonds.

Leaders in the conversion from cars to arms included Henry Ford, George Romney (coordinating the auto industry from peacetime to war production), GM's Wilson, and others, along with hardworking women riveting Chrysler tanks, Willow Run bombers, and the legendary Willys Jeep in Toledo. "Rosie the Riveter" placards were seen, depicting her as a poster child in the war effort. The sleeping giant of industrial America turned depression into hope through a mission of a proud nation; a patriotic drive that, through the grace of God, along with Winston Churchill and the brave British people, and other allies saved Western civilization. Radio messages from King

George VI provided much of the hope to survive the dark days of World War II. Our brave cousins in the British military (initially carrying on the battle for liberty against evil tyranny single-handedly) were joined later by our G.I Joes to change the balance of power in the world.

The United States of America emerged after World War II wounded but stronger, about to enter into a time of unprecedented financial expansion and world predominance. Our enemies in Japan and Germany became beneficiaries of the war; the Marshall Plan for Europe and General MacArthur's royal oversight in Japan provided postwar renewal. President Harry Truman's two "doomsday" bombs on the heartland of Japan brought about the end of hostilities. Opportunities for postwar economic and infrastructure investment resulted in a booming and prosperous USA.

As is well documented, Japan emerged over the years as the second most powerful and developed nation in the world (a spot relinquished to China in 2010), and along with a united Germany (after the Berlin Wall was dismantled) invested US aid dollars in developing auto industries of their own to challenge the Big Three of Detroit. Human nature, in many instances, does not cheer on super winners, even benevolent ones; soon the USA began to be envisioned by many as an imperialistic force to be challenged, not so much by countries with armies and tanks, but by those with weapons of mass destruction and cunning terrorism from without and secular humanists within the nation's political, academic, and entertainment circles of liberal influence.

CHAPTER 3

Returning to Birmingham and the early years of Ernest B. de Beaubien, we see in the 1940s and 1950s a time that was unparalleled in human history. At no other time or place in human history, since Adam and Eve, our first ancestors, were a relatively few persons so sheltered from a failing world than in the cubicles of Birmingham and like oases such as Chicago's North Shore, Shaker Heights, Ohio, and similar fortresses located in upscale New York, LA, and all major other cities. This, in addition to small towns and the rural American landscape, provided a brief moment of unprecedented tranquility. A peaceful time existed for a relatively few persons between the Second World War and the 1960s. Blessed—and not really aware of such a nanosecond of human existence—were the sheltered folk during those brief years. The world was collapsing all around, yet young Ernie, along with his counterparts in similar towns and cities all across the USA, experienced a never-before-existing, and perhaps not-to-return-again, point in time.

Along came TV: sitting for hours in front of test screens in order to catch a few moments of Howdy Doody Time or Uncle Miltie. Only a short time earlier a popular claim was heard that TV would never become reality; it was not possible to send pictures through the airways was the claim of many naysayers. But high-tech was approaching!

At times, a group of Ernie's friends would test fate by going downtown to buy baseball mitts at the Tool Shop or pegged pants from Hot Sam's, or venturing after dark into the popular Black and Tan clubs on John R. Street. Never fearing, for racial problems were not evident in those days. The 'Negro' welcomed whites that visited their entertainment enclaves. Black housekeepers and nannies rode the buses back and forth from Detroit to suburban homes each workday. Although seething internally, the racial explosion came only after the surreal days of the fifties. All changed forever with the LA riots and, closer to Ernie's home, the race riot on the once-peaceful Belle Isle and the burning of the Motor City in 1967.

But in the innocent early fifties, long, warm, Ernie's weekend nights were spent cruising chicks up and down Woodward Avenue and at Ross's Hollywood Drive-In. Cars coming in and out constantly, pausing only to ascertain the action and to order an occasional Coke (the liquid type, for there was no coke powder or similar mind-altering substances in those blessed days). Instead, Hank Williams' haunting song told the story as it was during balmy summer and autumn evenings: "Hey, good lookin', what ya got cookin'? ... I've got a hot-rod Ford and a two-dollar bill and I know a spot right over the hill where there's soda pop and the dancin's free."

The hot-rod Fords and Chevys cruised Woodward Avenue with Smitty or Brodie dual exhaust pipes screaming a nonverbal message of "Here I am, whatcha gonna do about it?" Driving their chopped and channeled hotrods were the gangs from Berkley with ducktail hairstyles and blue suede shoes, the uniform of the greasers. Preppies were identified as the opposing culture with their Princeton hairstyles, Levis, and white bucks. Drag races started from the red light at Thirteen Mile Road and continued to Fourteen Mile. The Royal Oak cops, in most cases, turned the other cheek to such innocent behavior that masked high school fears of the Bomb and the Korean War draft.

Weekends were also a time for sock hops featuring big bands with black musicians from Pontiac. Big Bill Turner's saxophone caused excited temps to rise for the dancing teens, while anxious temps rose in the chaperones; that long ago time a precursor to the mindless noise of the sixties and even more demonic noise after that. Maybe it was the weed or the snort that made the latter high-energy youth music tolerable to many. Maybe it was a revolution against the age of innocence. Who knows? Of course, the progeny of the sheltered didn't go to rock concerts that featured emaciated, long-haired types blaring their mind-numbing selections; instead it was Miss Brown's dance class at the Birmingham Community House: foxtrot, waltz, and later on when pushing the envelope, maybe Chubby Checkers and the Twist. These were happy days indeed for Ernie!

There were three teenage hangout drugstores in Birmingham, all situated on the corners of Woodward and Maple (Fifteen Mile road): Cunningham's, Wilson's, and Shain's. Actually,

Shain's was a little off Woodward on Maple and Pierce; to be had was the best soda fountain with twirling stools. This was the place to go on Saturday for lunch. A baloney and mayo sandwich along with maybe a cherry Coke and then a matinee flick at the Birmingham or Bloomfield Theaters. The choice of theater was based on the feature films for the day. If it was a good Western or action movie with Bogart or John Wayne, then great; if a love story with Victor Mature or Clark Gable, then nix. Either way it cost eleven cents to get in; shock set in when the price of a ticket was raised to twenty cents. This still left enough in one's pockets to buy a box of Jujubes. These were not primarily to chew, but to toss up to flicker in the light of the projector, to then land on the head of one of the Spalding saddle shoe-wearing girls in the front rows; hopefully on the one who was Ernie's crush of the moment.

High school Saturday evenings were times for sorority and fraternity meetings (these were the cliques naively thought to be extinct by the high school-carryings-on police). The boys would go to the homes of the sorority meetings after their own formal meetings ended (of the five based on the clique system prevailing among the students). Ernie generally moseyed over to the meeting home of the Betas. His potential dates were generally directed toward someone in Beta Beta Gamma. The Delta Beta Sigmmas were, for the most part, pretty and popular, but hung out mostly with Alpha Omega guys. Against this background of the times and places of falsely perceived reality lay the tug of eternal Truth that Ernie was at times seeking. A loving grandmother, aunt, and mother planted spiritual Truth seeds leading to a more permanent meaning. Ernie was a good boy in most respects in spite of sneaking smokes (tobacco, not grass) and minor indiscretions of the flesh. He was, after all, the recipient of valued religious instruction by Bill, his youth pastor along with the church's religious rituals of infant baptism, confirmation, and first communion. Walking successfully through these ecclesiastical hurdles meant there was no more to do, right? Graduation time! Nothing was mentioned about the New Testament Book of John chapter three, with its clear directive by Jesus that a spiritual, born-again experience of personal faith in Him, along with repentance was necessary for communion with God.

Some good works were evident in Ernie's life in the place of saving faith: his active membership in St. Andrew's Guild, a group of high school boys from Birmingham and also from Cranbrook (the exclusive Bloomfield Hills private boys' school), for instance. These acolytes handled altar candle lighting and processional-recessional chores at Sunday services at Christ Church Cranbrook, the cathedral in Bloomfield Hills. Ernie loved carrying a flag or the cross down the sanctuary aisle during Sunday services. He was certain at that time in life that his future resided within the church, raising a family, and doing good work for God.

In addition to church, much was instilled to help Ernie along his path of good works and eventual Truth. This was planted in him at Camp Hayo-Went-Ha, the state of Michigan YMCA camp on beautiful Torch Lake in Northern Lower Michigan. The director, Cliff "Cap" Drury, was a surrogate dad for a month each summer and remained a strong anchor and influence, even as Ernie drifted away from the shore of his worthy goals set for himself in high school.

CHAPTER 4

Satan, the Prince of Darkness, has plans of his own that are designed to attack individuals in various ways, depending on the moral and spiritual weaknesses of each person. Satan, who was once the top angel in God's host of angels, made the eternal error of choosing to compete with God Himself. The angel's name was Lucifer, the morning star. His punishment was to be separated from the heavenly host and exiled to Earth. Lucifer's name then became Satan (the Devil), and to this day he is spending his entire time and energy tormenting humankind. He does this by offering various enticing, ungodly temptations that are uniquely attractive to each individual. For a time his offerings can be very satisfying, whether it be alcohol, drugs, illicit sex, pride, or whatever else draws him or her in. But then, when a person is within Satan's grasp, he pulls the plug and turns the joy into an obsession. Addiction then suppresses all else for its fulfillment.

One of Ernie's weaknesses was with high school girls, and for a season this posed no problem to relationships, or life in general. What the boy did not realize at that point in his pilgrimage to God's Truth was that he thought he would find happiness in sensual pleasure, but really his hidden passion was to find an ideal woman he could love completely—rather than merely physical appearance.

At any rate, the struggle between right and wrong continued, with the wrong escalating. God could wait. Clever encouragement of Satan's demonic workers gave Ernie the desire to explore many enticing possibilities. But, as a member of the Birmingham High School graduating class of 1952 (the Crew of '52), Ernie got through that period in his life intact, but no closer to the Truth. It was on to university life with all the countless snares that milieu offers young, searching minds.

Very few places in the world are as beautiful in the autumn than the campus of Michigan State University in East Lansing. It is extraordinary to stroll the walks on the MSU campus, with every imaginable tree and plant to witness, along with appropriate tags identifying each species. It was especially lovely while listening to the chimes of the Beaumont Tower. Ernie savored every moment of this time, and all remained well throughout his freshman year at the then-named Michigan State College—taking in the sights and memories of the Spartans football team, coach Biggie Munn, and the Green and White. Oh yes, no coeds more beautiful than those at State, and Ernie took notice. Couples would stand closely entwined outside the women's dorms just before the residents had to comply with the then-strictly enforced curfews. And, there was fraternity life in anticipation for a bid from the house of choice; surviving hell week with comrades in the pledge class of Phi Delta Theta; as well as camaraderie with dorm roomies in East Shaw Hall. All in all, life was pretty much carefree and it lay before him in what seemed to be an endless voyage. Friday night sing fests with the other brothers along with a keg of beer made life for a brief moment an endless stream winding on into the future. No need to think too seriously about God; at least not now—plenty of time to do so later. However, even at these times, the small voice of God would creep in to his conscience.

The freshman year ended and a new chapter emerged when Ernie transferred to the University of Michigan in Ann Arbor for a planned study of pre-dentistry. This brought on an absolutely precious time. Ann Arbor is truly special, especially in the fall of the year. Walking hand in hand with one's sweetie with maple leaves turning gold and red, a warm autumnal breeze, and the anticipation of the Maize and Blue competing in the Big House—the country's largest stadium built by coach Fielding Yost and paid for by the great teams of H.O. "Fritz" Crisler and years later, Glenn Edward "Bo" Schembechler.

Ever since boyhood, Ernie would come to Ann Arbor with wide eyes and in awe, watching the great Wolverines of the golden era of college football. The team members in 1947 and 1948 were mostly returning World War II warriors who became equally dominating as the "Mad Magicians" of the gridiron. Howard Yerges, quarterback, field general, head magician, and coach H.O "Fritz" Crisler's second brain. Dick Rifenburg, Jack Weisenberger…"the spinning fullback," Pete and "Bump" Elliot, Bob Chappuis, Dick "Killer" Kempthorn, Len Ford, Bob Mann, J. T. White, Dom Tomasi and Alvin Wistert plugging the holes. The list of greats goes on. These were Ernie's heroes. Flashily reversing the ball around in the backfield from a single wing to the right formation was something to witness. Few on the opposition teams, or even Coach Crisler, were really aware where the ball was: double reverses, buck-reverse laterals, crisscrosses, quick-hits, and spins from many different formations. Michigan's 1947 team went on to clobber all comers, including archrival Ohio State 21–7. The season concluded by overpowering the University of Southern California in the Rose Bowl classic, 49–0.

Back from memory lane, Ernie's thoughts while watching the not as excellent, but still exciting, Wolverine teams of the 1950s gave rise to once again enjoying a time of blessing that he didn't quite take in or fully appreciate at the time. Win or lose in the classrooms, the weekend promised great times of the beer keg, his lovely Jeanne on his arm (by now having exchanged pins with a Kappa Kappa Gamma girl from a posh Chicago North Shore suburb), and an altered perception of life. Maybe so, but usually these times of instant gratification brought time in the bushes hurling beer previously quaffed in abundance. Sunday morning came soon enough with the previous evening's reminders of hangover and regrets. Maybe church next week; now certainly was not the time.

Later, engaged to the Kappa Kappa Gamma campus beauty, Ernie still gave little thought to anything past the here and now. A quick trip over to Canada in a friend's little MG automobile brought a memorable time spent at Menard's Tavern just outside Windsor, Ontario. All one cared to eat of the most delicious Lake Erie perch along with all the baked beans and cold slaw one could handle, washed down with Cincinnati

Cream Canadian beer ("who needs the handsome waiter") was the agenda for the evening.

The night ended with Tom and Ernie in a seat barely accommodating two, heading back to Ann Arbor and the books: music literature, psychology, and all the many business courses were enough to keep the here and now well intact. You see, the plan had changed from dentistry to business. Ernie's roomie was a pre-dent student and one look at the organic chemistry requirement for dentistry hopefuls was enough to deter Ernie from the rigors of that path of learning. Besides, business was more suited to his makeup as a people person. Sales! That was the future. Money! That was the goal. End life with the most toys. Maybe that is where truth was to be found?

For Ernie, major life crises came soon and heavy after earning his bachelor degree from the U of M, with no time to celebrate and savor the sweet smell of success in the completion of a rigorous course of instruction. Attending commencement exercises was passed over in favor of an early marriage, a real-world everyday work schedule, and settling into a life of organized stress. The wedding took place in a quiet Chicago North Shore village attended by various upscale personages behind surreal faces who came with well wishes and then soon departed.

The one thing recalled, time and again, from Ernie's long-term memory of the affair was the dour pastor who performed the ceremony; Doctor So-and-So. No part of the ceremony brought recollections other than that Ernie, the groom, made it through the ordeal. What memories that did remain centered on the prenuptial instruction provided by the good cleric. He issued forth a claim, with no Scriptural support, that Jesus' well-documented resurrection from the tomb is mythical. Why he chose to falsely expound on this topic in the context of marriage advising is a question that may never be answered.

Ernie's only thought at the time was that it was false teaching. The creeds and all the other religious head-knowledge gained at church as a youth were in direct opposition to the apostasy spewing forth from this so-called enlightener. Yet, not at all confident at that point in his pilgrimage, anxious to just get out of the parsonage as soon as possible, and in respect to his wife-to-be, Ernie let the statement slide by. But, in retrospect, carving out a major component in the heart of the gospel by a man of the cloth strengthened the Prince of Darkness's evil strategy by planting doubt in the youth's mind.

CHAPTER 5

During the next several years, Ernie traveled a dark road with many false turns and directions, but he also received blessings along the way. God spoke with His love and patience by the creation of two dear children, Katie and Angie, along with exciting entrepreneurial pursuits, and a winding road that ultimately would lead to the Highway of Holiness (Isaiah 35:8–10). But at this point, Satan was permitted by God to have the upper hand, as He had allowed in other lives and very much earlier with His servant Job (Job 1:12). Ernie, with unhealthy compulsions coupled with prideful self-centeredness, slipped deeper into a life leading inevitably to a dysfunctional existence. Balanced against the dark side were the blessings that God gave him that, in retrospect, held the keys to the eventual outcome of this narrative...Truth!

While every individual is born under curse brought on due to the original sin by Adam and Eve, some are influenced by God at an early age; such was the case with the older son in Jesus's parable of the two sons. He claimed to be obedient since an early age (Luke 15:29). However, God has different plans for His children according to His will for each. Some escape many of the harsh experiences of an unbelieving world and go on to lead pastoral lives; others along and at the opposite end of the spiritual continuum are meant to walk a different path. Saul of Tarsus, a highly educated man in the Mosaic Law and a leading overseer in the persecution and supervised murder of new followers of the risen Christ, was later visited in a vision by the risen Christ Himself, was baptized, and born again from above to eventually become the Apostle Paul (Acts chapter 9). Out of spiritual death came new life, as it did for the prodigal son in Jesus's parable (Luke 15:24).

Ernie's undergraduate degree from a nationally top-ranked BBA program might have led to the pursuit of an MBA; instead, he bore all he could take in terms of classroom rigors, and had no desire to ever enter another classroom. But with a newly minted Michigan business degree and the hope that resides in the heart of a young man bent on doing wonderful things in a life adventure stretching out into an unknown future, Ernie entered upon a career of marketing; first in the intangibles of investment securities. There was, during the mid-twentieth century, a certain romance in the selling of bonds. To do so, it inevitably involved a long internship building a sufficient clientele to support self and family, but it was a rewarding career that could bring satisfaction from the knowledge that one was engaged in an honorable profession. There is little need for kickbacks and other "added incentives" generally associated with industrial sales. One can fashion oneself as a gentleman, albeit an impoverished one. Later, Ernie developed a need and desire to bring to market novel surgical devices.

His first daughter, Katie, came into the world in the Chicago area where the de Beaubien family resided and Ernie was employed. Each day brought a new hope while riding on the clankety-clank elevated trains from Rogers Park past crowded apartment hovels and small industrial sweat shops on to the downtown Chicago loop and bustling LaSalle Street; skyscrapers, American and bank flags gloriously flapping in the breeze on handsome poles all along the busy street that terminated at the Chicago Board of Trade. Ernie's employ was with a local leading investment banking house that specialized in heading investment bank syndicates underwriting massive municipal Cook County bond issues and Illinois revenue obligations.

Summer was the scene of men wearing New Orleans-produced seersucker suits purchased at Marshall Field & Company or other emporiums lining State Street; jaunty straw hats with colorful head bands; regimental rep, school, or paisley designed ties; and two-tone winged tip oxfords. This pretty accurately described the uniform of the Street. It was difficult to ascertain if the frame the uniform covered was that of a highly successful investment house partner, a bank officer, a struggling up-and-coming securities salesman, or a bank clerk. A healthy number of "empty suits" also plied up and down the busy streets of Chicago's Loop—those with little between the ears but with crafty thoughts of effecting a con of one variety or another.

This was Chicago, as Carl Sandburg so accurately portrayed: "the husky, brawling, city of the big shoulders." Perhaps it was smaller than New York's Wall Street, but the magnates of LaSalle Street had no equal in terms of brash determination.

The Chicago Board of Trade controlled the bellies of America; pit traders screaming out buy and sell orders that ultimately determined the purchase prices of all sorts of commodities procured by shoppers in Main Street markets across the land.

The small de Beaubien family occupied a one-bedroom apartment high up in a well-placed building overlooking Lake Michigan and the Edgewater Beach Hotel. The apartment edifice was well over the hill in terms of its tenant dwellers, while the posh Edgewater Beach Hotel housing the famous Trader Vic's Polynesian restaurant was visible out his apartment window. For Ernie the Edgewater Beach was an establishment limited to strolling by and peering in. The family income covered the apartment rent of $165 monthly along with enough food on the table to exist from payday to payday, but with very few extras. Of course there were unlimited things to do on a Chicago Sunday afternoon that required little money: tall buildings, Grant Park, Navy Pier, strolling Oak Street Beach stretching out from the Drake Hotel and Lake Shore Drive. And, the de Beaubien's apartment building had a rooftop sun deck to leisurely drift off on while viewing the various female sun worshippers. Then there were the garlic and other kosher cooking aromas permeating the hallways every day along about dinnertime. Another Monday workday with the frustrations of a struggling investment securities broker lay a brief time ahead.

Something had to change! The family decided to move back to Detroit. Anyway, these were the glory days for the football Lions: Bobby Layne, Doak Walker, Joe Schmidt, the fearsome foursome consisting of Alex Karras and associates, along with the other great players that took the team to national championships. The baseball Tigers, on the other hand, were wallowing in mediocrity. But new young players in the likes of Al Kaline, "Stormin' Norman" Cash, Harvey Kuenn, Mickey Lolich, and others joined veterans such as George Kell to climb steadily until winning the great 1968 World Series.

But that was the future. In the meantime there were the watering holes in Palmer Park offering Ernie great steaks, gargantuan extra-dry rum martinis, and a variety of girls to visit with who sat on bar stools enjoying their nights after long days as clerks and receptionists in the myriad offices and warehouses of the city. Tempting bills of fare awaited should one choose to follow on the cross-roads traveled in life.

CHAPTER 6

Shortly after returning to the Motor City, Ernie became frustrated with his slow progress in the investment securities business and, at the same time, was overcome with a passion to go into the business of marketing surgical products. Gazing into his home's crackling fireplace one winter evening, the decision was made. New directions were initiated by the forming of a partnership with a university friend. Partnerships are the worst possible form of business relationships, due to the unlimited personal liability emanating from all the partners' actions. This came to haunt Ernie, but while working together the two partners became distributors of a focused line of operating room specialties, including surgical sutures, ligatures, instruments, scalpel blades, and so forth. After a while it became clear that the partnership was going nowhere. Ernie bought out his partner and continued to sell the line to hospitals in Lower Michigan and environs. In the process he learned how to fly, purchased an airplane, and developed the business as a sole proprietor.

Too much time away from home and family, along with constant occupational stress, put a strain on Ernie. This, then, caused our boy to walk further down the road leading away from Truth. At that point in time, his definition of truth was the pursuing of material rewards and that remained his focus for several years, only to grow with each career conquest.

Meanwhile, his wife was struggling with, and yielding to, her own set of iniquities in the grossly abusive use of prescription drugs and alcohol. The family broke up under the strain, yet Ernie's love and caring for his daughters grew even stronger. God was responsible for keeping the young entrepreneur from complete disarray. But new surgical specialties were developed, leading to new strains on every aspect of Ernie's life and spiritual health.

Ernie's now former wife, due to free will and satanic attacks, became incompetent to care for the family's children. She drifted back and forth from alcohol treatment centers in a continued tragic life of substance addiction. She was fighting her own set of demons, thus Ernie eventually took custody of the girls. This brought back control to his life.

However, one compulsion was replaced with another: The desire to make it really big in terms of monetary rewards became his new master. A paraphrase of Scripture states that if the love of money is the driving force in life, one will surely wander away from faith (1 Timothy 6:10). This was Ernie's new sin of choice, and given the right set of circumstances, material success would continue to control his life. God would not be honored. In the twisted logic of someone in such a position, the reasoning is, who needs God?

Fortunately, God did not give up on him. Several life-threatening instances, including close calls when flying his plane around the country, spared his physical life. God had work for Ernie, and His plan did not include the pursuit of material treasure. While Ernie did not obtain material financial independence, the surgical products brought to market, in collaboration with an inventive and innovative surgical nurse, went on to be of human value; the devices were, and still are, utilized in many hospitals.

For years he pondered the reasons for not reaping great material rewards when they seemed right at his fingertips to be grasped, but later he realized God's design and will in the matter. The products were meant to be available for the good they would do, but God had other plans for Ernie himself. He was beginning to get a shadowy glimpse into knowing God. So, he abandoned his dream of material abundance and started down a new roadway. Still, Ernie was not turning from the material to the spiritual.

He was remarried by now, and his new wife, Fran, was a very talented singer and up-and-coming Nashville songwriter who came to accept Jesus into her heart as Savior, and soon afterward by Holy Spirit, led Ernie to the Lord. This marriage lasted for over thirty years, only to end in tragic and painful multiple health issues for his wife. The silver lining was that the final years of her life provided an opportunity for Ernie's unending attention and care to her. For once in his shallow life, Ernie placed the needs and comfort of another before his own. While it was a sad parting the last day and night of Fran's life, it was also a celebration of the beginning of her next life adventure. An angel of the Lord came to her to accompany her to paradise. Her final prayer after hours of private conversation with God was "Hurry, Jesus."

Ernie had been given a second chance to serve his wives. Years earlier, the first wife was trapped in addictions, but Ernie was not mature enough to provide what was needed. This was reversed with Fran, as he did all he could in his very humble way for her in the last years of her life.

Ernie accepted Jesus in their small Detroit apartment by the help of Fran and the powerful wooing of Holy Spirit. There were others who planted seeds of eternal Truth in his mind. There were media evangelists, Billy Graham being the foremost, but also others. One inwardly beautiful person was the purchasing contact Ernie would visit every week or two for orders at the institution where she was employed. She would be sitting at her desk with a Holy Bible open in front of her as "our know-it-all" salesman came for the sales call. She would read to Ernie from the Book before any business was discussed. This irritated Ernie, but with eyes on receiving a purchase order, he tolerated the protocol. Then, after several weeks of this, amazingly enough he actually started to look forward to Mrs. Perkins's Bible sessions with him. Of course he was still interested primarily in receiving the sales order, but he was grateful for hearing the Word of God.

As mentioned, his wife did complete the harvest of the ripe fruit from the tree, and through the urging of Holy Spirit, Ernie prayed for forgiveness and accepted Jesus as his personal Lord and Savior in December 1979 (John 1:12).

As the Bible promises, when a person repents and accepts Christ by faith, the old is gone and all things become new. Born again! **"Therefore if any man is in Christ, he is a new creature; the old things passed away; behold new things have come"** (2 Corinthians 5:17). New birth! The beginning of Truth! Returning to God is the meaning of life. All people search for this Truth, whether realizing it or not. Some rely on religion, but that won't save. Being a good person and doing good deeds can't save. No church denomination can save. Only Holy Spirit can draw a sinner—and that includes everyone. **"All have sinned and fall short of the glory of God"** (Romans 3:23).

CHAPTER 7

The evidence of conversion to new spiritual birth from above is evident in oneself, and evident to others in various ways at various times. In many new Christians, the evidence of change takes place gradually; in others the evidence, both outward and inward, is immediate and explosive. Whether gradual or dramatic, certain phenomena are bound to occur, if the acceptance of Christ is genuine. An individual is able to determine if the accepting of Jesus as Savior and Lord represents a new direction in life, or if the experience is an empty confession to satisfy others, or merely for outward show. Genuine new spiritual birth is created by Holy Spirit and accompanied by repentance (Acts 2:38). For some, this involves a long walk back to God; for others it is in an instant, but in all cases there is a moment in time when the choice is made to accept Christ as the way to enjoy communion with the heavenly Father. Truth!

Although it is an older, somewhat intimidating theological term not understood by all, *repentance* can be defined as a change in heart leading to a transformed mind and life (Romans

12:2). Yes, Jesus is our Savior, but He is also Lord in a converted person's individual life. In addition to repentance, newborn faith is to be shared with others through Christian baptism.

"It came about in those days that Jesus came from Nazareth in Galilee, and was baptized by John in the Jordan. And immediately coming up out of the water, He saw "the heavens opening, and the Spirit like a dove descending upon Him" (Mark 1:9–10). In this passage we have the Son of God Himself being baptized as an example for all to follow. As the Christ, He certainly didn't need baptism, but this was the moment of the commencement of His earthly ministry and the man, Jesus, needed the blessing of His Father. This was witnessed by Holy Spirit's descent from Heaven. Then, at the end of His ministry, Jesus gave His followers the charge for their continued ministry to be accomplished after He ascended back to heaven. **"All authority has been given to Me in heaven and on earth. Go therefore and make disciples of all the nations, baptizing them in the name of the Father and the Son and the Holy Spirit, teaching them to observe all that I commanded you; and lo, I am with you always, even to the end of the age"** (Matthew 28:18–20). The Great Commission from our Lord includes the charge to baptize others.

Luke authored a narrative of Jesus's ministry in his gospel account, and also the continued ministry of Christ's disciples in Acts. The combined words of Luke, a gentile physician, in these two books account for the lengthiest testimony to Jesus by any of the New Testament writers. Writing about Peter, Luke quotes the apostle as follows: **"Repent, and let each of you be baptized in the name of Jesus Christ for the forgiveness of** your sins; and you will receive the gift of the Holy Spirit" (Acts 2:38). Peter also urged the following in his first epistle: **"Corresponding to that, baptism now saves you–not the removal of dirt from the flesh, but an appeal to God for a good conscience–through the resurrection of Jesus Christ"** (1 Peter 3:21). Water has no power to save, but baptism in water is a profession of faith in the resurrection of Jesus as the Son of God and the decision to walk with Him as Lord. Luke also wrote the following: **"And Philip opened his mouth, and beginning from this Scripture [Isaiah 53: 7ff] he preached Jesus to him ... and the eunuch said, 'Look! Water! What prevents me from being baptized?' And Philip replied, 'If you believe with all your heart, you may.' And he answered and said, 'I believe that Jesus Christ is the Son of God.' And they both went down into the water, Philip as well as the eunuch; and he baptized him"** (Acts 8: 35–38). The apostle Paul provides the following words of assurance: **"Or do you not know that all of us who have been baptized into Christ Jesus have been baptized into His death? Therefore we have been buried with Him through baptism into death, in order that as Christ was raised from the dead through the glory of the Father, so we too might walk in newness of life. For if we have become united with Him in the likeness of His death, certainly we shall be also in the likeness of His resurrection"** (Romans 6:3–5).

Paul, himself, was baptized by immersion subsequent to his conversion on the road to Damascus (Acts 9:18).

Ernie de Beaubien, in obedience to God's Word, was baptized not long after accepting Jesus as Lord and Savior. The event took place on Orchard Lake. One leaves Birmingham and winds along pristine roadways that lead to an area with many small lakes. Ernie drove with anticipation past Long and Pine Lakes, enjoying the beauty of summer. It was a beautiful day. The sun shone brightly on Orchard Lake and upon those who were immersed in the lake with him, including his wife. All were filled with promises of glad tidings while praising God in prayer and song. There was a good deal of activity on the lake that day, with a mixture of gleaming white and brilliantly colored sails capturing breezes to transport a variety of hulls back and forth between sleek aluminum and the more classic wooden Chris-Craft motor boats.

The baptizer that day requested that all to be immersed share an appropriate Scripture verse with the witnesses standing on the bank of the lake. Ernie was led to share the following passage: "'Come now, and let us reason together,' says the Lord. Though our sins are as scarlet, they will be as white as snow; though they are red like crimson, they will be like wool" (Isaiah 1:18).

Then the following question was asked: "Who do you believe Jesus to be?" With all his heart, Ernie's reply was "The Son of God." Then he was immersed into the cool water.

A few days later, Pastor Richard inquired about what Ernie was going to do now. The question referred to what ministry Ernie would start preparing for, as service was evidence of faith (Ephesians 2:10; James: 2:17)—service rendered to others being the rent we pay for the space occupied while here on earth. And the ways of serving are unending: for example, encouragement, mission work, music, teaching, visitation, youth work, parachurch volunteerism, and so forth. We do what we do well by employing a spiritual gift or gifts that God supplies to all believers at the moment of new birth.

    The Bible refers to all believers when referring to ministering priests, not just an elect hierarchy. **"You also, as living stones, are being built up as a spiritual house for a holy priesthood"** (1 Peter 2:5, 9). The priesthood of all believers was practiced throughout the apostolic age. It was not until the Ante-Nicene period of Christian church history that the clergy–laity separation surfaced. The Greek Church started a hierarchy of patriarchs, while the Roman church went further by producing the papal monarchy in the Middle Ages. This culminated with the pope being declared the universal and infallible bishop in the Vatican Council in 1870. Many other denominational groups, as well, have elaborate clerical hierarchies. While this practice may be in agreement with church denominational tradition and polity, it is nowhere to be found in biblical teaching.

CHAPTER 8

In contemplating his pastor's inquiry regarding service, Ernie's thoughts went back to the days of his youth, walking along skid row on the way to watch the Detroit Tigers play, and experiencing the pull of his heart at seeing the fallen men trapped in their prisons of despair. God recalled his memories back to those days, and he made the decision to go down again to skid row, newly centered in the Cass Corridor. The Detroit Rescue Mission was located there, founded on a vision received by the Rev. Stuckey seventy years earlier. Having moved a few times to remain close to the clientele, it was currently located in a multipurpose building on Third Street and in 2012 marked one hundred years in existence.

Ernie offered his service as a volunteer to the mission while still in business as vice president of a local distribution firm. Upon meeting with Will, the director of the Detroit Rescue Mission, it was agreed that Ernie's business and communication background fit well with the mission's current need for someone to spearhead fund development efforts to corporate, financial, and other business organizations. This led a year later to a staff position that included, in addition to fund development, preaching and counseling residents of the mission.

The skin color of the men entering each day for food and shelter had changed since the Great Depression days; now, older white faces were mostly replaced by younger black faces. Chronic drunks were in many cases replaced by, or were in addition to, drug addicts of one sort or another. One young man came into the mission stoned and grasping for his last chance at life. After going through delousing procedures, Rob lay in a state of near-unconsciousness on the floor at the back of the chapel for six weeks. He was just coherent enough to take in sustenance and to mentally process God's Word spoken by evangelists preaching at the three daily gospel services. Through Holy Spirit's working in Rob's mind and heart, he survived and eventually accepted Christ. This one-time drug dealer, every week earning thousands of dollars dealing to the youth of the inner-city housing projects, was eventually hooked himself with Satan's products of death and destruction. After repenting of his depraved life style, he was cleansed and, instead of dealing drugs to the youth of the neighborhood, would witness to them with his life as a living example. He was a remarkable street evangelist and his health and ministry were both blessed greatly. Ernie was privileged to have had the opportunity to disciple Rob and others in the basics of Christianity.

At the time of Ernie's service at the Detroit Rescue Mission, he was filled with a deep need to learn more about God. This led him to completing a biblical course of study from the venerable Moody Bible Institute of Chicago. Once again, his past led to the reality of God's plan for his present and future. He recalled walking along LaSalle Street as a junior investment securities salesman and viewing with an unexplained sense of captivation the entrance plaque to the Moody Bible Institute. This occurred several times and made a lasting impression; the memory now brought to mind a similar unexplainable feeling as he had as a boy when gazing on the down-and-outers on skid row. He had an identical spiritual draw to the two experiences, and thus the decision to enroll at MBI to learn more about God's Truth.

It became evident through his studies that while salvation is at the very core of faith development, there are other benefits added to the promise in Matthew 11:28 of salvation rest. These other benefits can be likened to those of an employee working for a salary. Many large and small organizations provide benefits in addition to salary for their employees. In fact, it is thought that in recent times a great majority of larger employers provided some form of health insurance to their employees; however this percentage has no doubt lessened due to the recent Great Recession of 2008 and years following. Health insurance was a safety net in times of need to Ernie and his family. And while these benefits are greatly appreciated by the recipients, they are temporary.

Conversely, believers will cherish forever God's benefits package added to His salvation rest. It was the apostle Peter, as many know, who was among the inner circle of Christ's disciples. It was he who Jesus addressed when He stated, **"You are Peter, and upon this rock I will build My church; and the gates of Hades will not overpower it"** (Matthew 16:18). And although Peter denied the Lord at a time of fear and weakness just prior to his Master's death, his fellowship with Christ was later wonderfully restored. It was Peter who stood on the street in Jerusalem on the first Christian Pentecost and courageously proclaimed the gospel of Christ. Some three thousand people responded to his Spirit-filled message, received Christ as their Savior, and were baptized in the Holy Spirit.

Peter later authored a message of salvation communicated to him by Holy Spirit (1 Peter 1:1–5). He began with a greeting to a group of new Christians, reminding them that they were aliens and strangers in this world in which they lived. He specifically addressed those who were scattered throughout five provinces of Asia Minor. Three of these provinces were represented when Peter preached on that day of Pentecost: Pontus, Cappadocia, and Asia. Galatia is mentioned (Acts 16:6) as having been visited by Paul and his companions. Paul established churches in Galatia and later wrote an urgent and instructive letter to the Galatians as preserved in the New Testament canon of Scripture. Paul and his companions also attempted to minister in Bithynia, but Holy Spirit directed them elsewhere (Acts 16:7–10).

The aliens to whom Peter is writing are strangers in a greater sense than just geographically. Peter is speaking about a deep meaning of being a Christian; the King is Christ, and His followers reside in heaven. The writer of Hebrews 11:13 states that we are all strangers and pilgrims, exiles on the earth. Additionally, Paul wrote in Philippians 3:20 that our true citizenship is in heaven. But while sojourning on this foreign land, the believer is able to communicate, through prayer, with heaven. Communication within human dyads involves a two-way process requiring the producer of a message and the interpretation and action by the receiver of the message to complete the transaction. In the case of salvation, both the divine offering and the human acceptance of God's grace are involved in the two-way process.

Peter wrote in his first epistle about three specific statements concerning God's two-way communication with us that involve the tri-unity of God: Father, Son, and Holy Spirit. First, we are chosen by God to obey Jesus Christ (1 Peter 1:2). Obedience is at the very heart of His communication design for us. Second, we are chosen according to the foreknowledge of God. God knows everything, past, present, and future. Third, we are chosen by the sanctifying work of the Spirit (1:2). We are strangers in this world. With the leading of the Holy Spirit, Ernie separated himself from the worldly system that is in total opposition to the things of the Spirit. We are sprinkled with Jesus's blood, signifying the personal application to us of the sacrifice of Christ (1:2).

Mercy (1 Peter 1:3) is a key word that needs to be understood in order to grasp the fullest meaning of Peter's teaching about God's communication to us. Salvation is not achieved by human effort, but comes through God's mercy. As Paul wrote: **"According to His mercy, He saved us"** (Titus 3:5).

CHAPTER 9

Ernie's new spiritual birth was the beginning of a new life in Christ. The wondrous gift of a new birth is eternal life; but as referred to briefly above, there are also wonderful fringe benefits (1 Peter 1:3–5). God's eternal benefits, in addition to new spiritual life, include the following:

A Living Hope (1:3). God promises to each of us that we have a living hope that is not dependent upon our environment or outward circumstances. The word *living* means dynamic, vital, alive. This hope is like living waters flowing from a perennial stream that never runs dry. Such hope comes from the very source of God Himself. The word *hope* is uniquely Christian and has meaning only because of the resurrection of Christ. Peter goes on to say that because God raised Christ from the dead we are given over to faith and hope (1:21). We ought to believe so deeply that we live this hope, ready to give an answer to the person who asks us the reason for our hope. We should live this hope so that it shows itself to others, so they will ask why we are so hopeful (1 Peter 3:15). This is powerful, lifestyle evangelism!

A Heavenly Inheritance. The new spiritual birth not only provides eternal hope, but also guarantees our forever retirement program by a heavenly inheritance. This inheritance has four outstanding features (1:4). First, our heavenly inheritance is *imperishable,* meaning that the inheritance is incorruptible. It cannot be destroyed by the whims of financial markets or economic and political events. Imperishable is the same Greek word used in Romans 1:23 in describing the glory of the incorruptible God. This is in contrast to corruption that permeates man's political and social systems and constantly endangers personal inheritances. There is a human frailty that grows and grows with the passing of time, as witnessed in all the economies and countries of the world from the dictatorial despots to the much lesser invasiveness of many democracies. Even within the Unites States, the uniquely blessed republic formed under guidance by God in answer to the call for freedom from monarchal rule, we see an ever-greater grasp of individual freedoms by politicians, accompanied by the weakening of worldly inheritances. Spending far beyond the capability to pay for the excesses made the nation a debtor to China and other creditor economies. This not only limits the flexibility to make political and economic decisions, but also endangers future financial security of individual inheritances.

Second, our inheritance is *undefiled*, meaning unpolluted and fresh. It will never spoil or decay due to worldly ecological occurrences. Global warming gurus promote all sorts of gloom and doom scenarios; whether or not their prognoses are based on facts remains to be learned as events play themselves out.

What is known in certainty is that God's inheritances are and will remain undefiled.

Third, they will *not fade away,* remaining bright and vital. Even the strongest and brightest of humankind's masterpieces fade with time. The Statue of Liberty is the essence of lasting greatness and beauty. Our nation spent millions to restore it, but it still needs additional restoration. Experts are also attempting to bring back a fading *Mona Lisa* and other works of art. The heavenly inheritance that our God provides for us will never fade.

And fourth, this inheritance is *reserved for us* in heaven. The word reserved can be translated to guard or to keep. This is the promise of God. He will guard, keep, and reserve our heavenly inheritance for those who have received the free gift of salvation that He offers to all who accept His Son. Grab on to and hold your reserved ticket to heaven with all trust, as it will be honored on the express trip to paradise at any moment of time in the future. Many hoping to see an exciting football game might have their ticket not honored due to a snow country-arena roof collapse or seats not ready for use at a decisive athletic event, as was evidenced just prior to the Super Bowl game in Dallas several years ago. Or, how about the poor bloke who was on vacation from Northern Michigan and had good reserved seats to watch the Tigers play the Yankees. It was the last day of his vacation, and the game was called on account of rain. Not so with God! Hang on with full faith, as your reservation on the heaven-bound express will be honored whenever it is your time to climb on board.

Protected by the power of God (v. 5). We are protected by the power of God, not the Securities and Exchange Commission. Much more secure! Until the day we claim our inheritance, God promises to provide a living hope for us to shield us with His power. We will not lose our inheritance due to dishonest or faulty management. There are no 401k debacles or Ponzi schemes in God's retirement package.

Salvation with all its benefits is God's greatest gift, yet it is just the beginning of His manifestation of love; the spiritual blueprint for faith development is also provided by God's grace. It is by faith that we live day by day (Galatians 3:11). There is an ongoing battle between good and evil, both on a global scale in the playing out of latter-day prophecy in the Middle East and elsewhere, and in a micro sense within us. Ernie fought many battles within himself, but God is to be praised above all words as He protected him and offered supreme patience.

But there is only so much time, and no one knows how much is to be allowed before the opportunity for choosing ends. We have been given free will to choose our destiny. Will your choice be light or darkness, life or death? The time for selecting one's eternal place of residence for eternity is limited. Will it be a dwelling in the most beautiful place beyond all comprehension of beauty with God, or will it be in the company of Satan in eternal darkness and depravity? The apostle Paul instructed us to use the shield of faith to extinguish the flaming arrows of the evil one (Ephesians 6:16). The key is to take advantage of God's *power:* **"For God has not given us a spirit of timidity, but of power and love and discipline"** (2 Timothy 1:7).

What a momentous time the Day of the Lord will be when the redeemed are caught up to accompany Christ on His earthly descent to Earth as King of King and Lord of Lords (2 Thessalonians 2:1). Until that day we have not been left alone, as the Helper, the Holy Spirit, is present as the divine tutor and implementer of God's design for faith and life (John 14:26). Ernie's quest for Truth led him, by the hand of the Holy Spirit, to a faith development stemming from salvation. Ernie's probe led him to the words of Peter (2 Peter 1:1–11). The treatise on faith development is available for all in learning of God's promises and process.

CHAPTER 10

Faith is a hard word to properly define in relation to personal life application. We may have a general idea of what faith is, but do we really grasp its meaning? Do we fully understand the divine potential that true faith offers each believer? We are able to grasp the true meaning of faith by looking at God's promises. To follow God's design, it is important to first grasp the promise. The great apostle Peter was thought to be an old man when he dictated his second letter. His thoughts drifted back to his early years. In the greeting to the letter, in the second letter of Peter, he addressed his readers in verse one by the familiar name of his youth: Simon or Simeon. It is the form that is the most distinctively Jewish. He then joins the old name with the new name, Peter, which the Lord Jesus gave him. The name means rock, and the two combine Jewish and Christian associations—old and new covenants.

Peter describes himself as a bondservant. The Greek word here implies more than merely a servant, per se. It literally means a slave. A bondservant is purchased with a price like any slave to do the work of the master. However, instead of being bought with money, the price for a Christian bondservant was Christ's own sacrifice. There is another Greek noun for servant, diakonos, describing ministers and deacons. It is commonly used in the New Testament, but in this instance it is not used, but rather the word for bondservant, doulos, is.

In addition to Peter, there are instances in the New Testament where doulos is used to describe various bondservants of Christ. Also, those who are to be with God and Christ Jesus forever are identified as being bondservants (Revelation 22:3–6). Peter's work as a bondservant of Christ was that of an apostle, one sent out as a missionary into the world to attract souls to Christ through the ministry of Holy Spirit. In calling oneself a bondservant of Christ, as many of those early church leaders did, and we do if we truly are such, we do so as one who formerly was a bondservant of Satan. Now, having been bought by Christ through His sacrifice, we are now willing slaves of our new Master. There is no vacuum or third position in this life. We are able to serve only one master, whether it is Satan or Christ.

It appears that a reason for Peter to write this epistle was for us to hang on to our faith. We must resist the evil one and his false teachers and keep on following Jesus. Faithfulness is of the highest priority in Christian discipleship. Temptation is the tool Satan uses to diminish faith. Even after his spiritual new birth, Ernie was tempted at various times while growing in his faith. This is true for most Christian. But, through the indwelling of Holy Spirit, believers have the strength to overcome temptation before it explodes into sin (1 Corinthians 10:13).

As Peter's life was coming to a close, he had a clear understanding of who he was and who his Master was. He walked humbly with the Lord. He speaks with authentic humility as one who followed Jesus for many years. After leaving much of his past life to follow Jesus, he became one in the inner circle of disciples. He failed the Lord miserably by denying Him at a time of great need, but was then a witness to the resurrected Christ and experienced his own spiritual renewal at the first day of Christian Pentecost. He was baptized by the Holy Spirit and preached with power to the crowd. He later served as an elder in the early church as it spread throughout the world, and was now ministering to a suffering church—as he himself was preparing for a martyr's death. Indeed, he walked humbly with God.

His second letter was written to fellow bondservants of Christ. This is the common denominator that brings true believers together. It is correct to interpret Peter's statement in (2:1) as an attribute of God, righteousness being His just and holy dealing with men and women. This is God' design; this is how He communicates with us. In His righteousness He bestows the same precious faith in all who come back to Him through Christ. There is also a strong statement in (2:1) authenticating the deity of Christ. The strict grammatical construction of this passage attributes both God and Savior to Jesus. The word "our" properly comes before God, not between the words God and Savior. The literal rendering of the first verse is: **our God and Savior Jesus Christ**, not our God and our Savior Jesus Christ.

Peter goes on to tell us that the knowledge of God is the means by which grace and peace are communicated to the soul. This comes through a knowledge given to us by God in His written Word, the Scriptures, and in His Living Word, Jesus, who is the Word of God (John 1:1). We connect this knowledge in verse two with verse three.

> "...His divine power has granted us everything pertaining to life and godliness, through the true knowledge of Him [Christ] who called us..."

God has given us all the things that are necessary for our salvation: Grace and peace are ours–if we seek after the knowledge God has given to us. Notice it is in the past tense. God has granted to us everything pertaining to life and godliness. His divine power in verse three has been granted to all bondservants of Jesus Christ.

Bible teaching urges us to live by that power that comes to us through the knowledge of Jesus. Our glorification, of course, will not be complete until our homecoming to the Lord, yet we have been granted His divine power and nature, that is, all things necessary for life and godliness. Holy Spirit, who indwells all believers, is working to complete our divine nature. Let's not resist His work by drawing back to our old natures. Verse four continues this theme. "He has granted to us His precious and magnificent promises..." (Notice again this is past tense). The promises of God are precious and great.

Peter's words here might be seen as overly bold, yet they do not go beyond other statements of Holy Scripture. At the beginning God said "Let Us make man in Our image, according to Our likeness..." (Genesis 1:26). Also, Paul tells us that

"But we all, with unveiled face, beholding as a mirror the glory of the Lord, are being transformed into the same image from glory to glory, just as from the Lord, the Spirit" (2 Corinthians 3:18). Further, the words of John: **"...now we are children of God, and it has not appeared as yet what we shall be. We know that when He appears, we shall be like Him, because we shall see Him just as He is. And everyone who has this hope fixed on Christ purifies himself, just as He is pure"** (1 John 3:2, 3).

God's precious promises enable the Christian to become partakers of the divine nature and to escape from corruption. As with all great Truths in the Bible, we see that a partnership is involved between God and humankind, between God's providence and our free will. In these beautiful words of Peter in his second letter we have heard God's promises that our faith can develop to the point that our nature mirrors that of Christ. His divine nature and power have been granted to us—granted to us in order to provide us with everything we need for eternal life and godliness as we walk on the highway of holiness from God's promises to life's application.

CHAPTER 11

Transferring faith theology to life application involves two steps, as stated in 2nd Peter verse seven. First, developed godliness is applied in brotherly kindness. The Living Bible paraphrases it, "This will make possible the next step, which is to enjoy other people and to like them."

Brotherly kindness is very special. The Greek word is the familiar word *philadelphia*, and really means affection toward fellow believers, our brothers and sisters in Christ. We ought never to be strangers with other believers. This is evident when visiting other churches where we do not know anyone. Missionaries claim this is particularly true, even when there are dissimilar language and cultural barriers. The Apostle Paul encourages transferring theory into action; in 1 Thessalonians 5:11 he urges:

"Therefore encourage one another and build up one another..." Building up is so needed in the extreme bitterness experienced in our 21st century world. Not a day goes by without the media reporting terrible deeds that humans inflict on one another; further, most brutal acts go unreported. Some are motivated through ambition, jealousy, or hatred; however, a recent new form of violence has emerged. Satan has devised a new dimension of demonic savagery: acts of brutality set in motion through trivial miscommunication or irritations of one sort or another. Even a glance wrongly interpreted can prompt violent responses. Indeed, some acts are triggered for no apparent reason at all. There are new and frightening twists: drive-by shootings, hassling those of different ethnic, cultural, lifestyle, racial, or religious backgrounds, as well as the disabled and the elderly, and road rage. None of us are exempt from these new forms of obscenity. We witness this treachery at ever-younger ages with the epidemic of youth shootings and beatings.

Whether destructive acts are perpetuated against others in an instant with a gunshot or slowly through emotional control or abuse, miscommunication drives these actions. Christ is the answer, and His model is the one to emulate in all communicative transactions. Gentleness and thoughtfulness are the guides to follow in personal contacts and relationships. Brotherly kindness is a wonderful quality between persons. There is, however, a deeper quality of faith that knows no limits and has no conditions (2 Peter 1:7). It is love (agape), or the very quality of God's love. This is the final step in the development of human faith, short of glorification received upon entering our heavenly adventure. This love, agape, is the greatest of all Christian graces: (1 Corinthians 13:13), and is the apex of faith development. Vine's Expository Dictionary of Old and New Testament Words defines agape: "This is the word most characteristic of Christianity."

What exactly is this thing called love that Peter is writing about? Everybody talks and writes about love; just about every song on secular media is related to the subject of love in one way or another. The same is true of television and the big screen. There is an underlying self-centeredness that permeates counterfeit love; certainly it was the case with Ernie in all of his searching years. A shallow form of love was shown in public and private relationships. And there is support for this mentality. Western culture is dedicated to the "god" of physical love. This is depicted in Madison Avenue's mirroring of culture's addiction to the worship of physical perfection and youth; to political leaders elected primarily on charismatic attributes and deceptive promises.

There is an epidemic of counterfeit love from those willing to sell body and soul in the perversion of God's gift of beauty; the more physically attractive purveyors and those skilled in counterfeit love products are able to attract an upscale clientele starving for emotional affection. Witness the darker side of massive professional athletics party venues, where young prostitutes successfully ply their trade to those searching (unknowingly) for authentic love and affection. Satan's offerings, while promising instant gratification, provide instead only emptiness and continued searching down the road to despair. To use God's gifts of physical beauty in a perverted way is so sad.

As Ernie discovered with blinding clarity, authentic love given selflessly is blessed by the greatest and most genuine love in return. God knew the circumstances. After the passing of two wives; the first after thirty-one years, the second after only fifteen months, he met Lorna, the woman destined to be one in mind and body according to God's plan designed for each of them.

There was an instantaneous friendship that developed into a spiritual and intellectual bonding culminating in marriage. This time around Ernie was, for the first time in his life, consumed with giving rather than receiving. True love is the epitome of faith development, God's love for them and their love for others (cf. 1 John). It is impossible to love in excess, and the more we give the more is returned, this being entirely opposite to the world's view of get more and give less. But sometimes it takes a long while to realize this truth. Sometimes it takes a lifetime. Ernie thanked God that it was not too late to do so. After bringing Ernie and Lorna together in love and a partnership of faith, Ernie came under the comfort and instruction of Holy Spirit. Ernie's quest for God's Truth continued with faith development at the highest grace, which is agape love. The most simple and profound definition of agape in all literature is simply this: "**... for God is love**" (1 John 4:8). It is the highest expression of love and the ultimate goal of any Christian. By this expression, one is recognized as a disciple of Christ (John 13:35).

This characteristic attribute expresses ideas previously unknown in the world, either in the secular or theological literature. It is uniquely a New Testament revelation by divine revelation of Holy Spirit. It describes God's communication of love toward His Son (John 17:26), toward the human race generally (John 3:16; Romans 5:8), and toward believers (John 14:21). Love is listed first as a fruit of Holy Spirit (Galatians

5:22), and expresses itself first of all in obedience to Christ's commandments:

"Beloved, let us love one another, for love is from God; and everyone who loves is born of God and knows God. The one who does not love does not know God, for God is love" (1 John 4:7–8). Daniel Meyer wrote the following story illustrating such a love:

It was an ordinary day of commuting for Cameron Hollopeter. The 20-year-old film student made his way down the steps into a New York City subway station to wait for the train. All of a sudden, something went horribly wrong in the young man's brain, sending him into a violent seizure. Hollopeter fell to the ground, got back up again, and began stumbling along the edge of the subway platform. Moments later, he tumbled down onto the railway bed, just as the rumbling of an approaching train began to shake the station. No one managed to capture the moment on video, but we know how the people in the subway probably reacted. Some turned away, eyes clenched against the horror of what was happening. Other commuters stood frozen in a sense of utter helplessness. Others were in such a hurry to get to where they needed to go, that they missed the moment altogether.

In mere seconds, a young man with dreams of becoming a Hollywood producer would meet an unthinkably violent end, and no one could stop it. No one *would* stop it…except the one man who did. A 50-year-old construction worker named Wesley Autrey did the unthinkable. This middle-aged black man from Harlem who had little in common with a white

Harvard student, chose to do what no one else at that scene elected to do; he chose to cross over.

Autrey strode across that subway platform, jumped down into the ditch, and covered Hollopeter's bloodied, writhing body with his own. He held Hollopeter against the ground while the subway train thundered over them.

Later, when interviewed about the incident, Autrey said that when he saw the headlights of the No. 1 train appear, he knew he had to make a split decision. "I don't feel like I did something spectacular; I just saw someone who needed help." He said: "I did what I felt was right—we're supposed to come to rescue people."

There's something about the story of Autrey and Hollopeter that is both inspiring and convicting. It's like there's a law of love—a law of profound regard for others— which, if followed by all, would make this world a very different place than it is. It is not just clear why the commuters did what they did. Perhaps they were just hardened by the ways of the world—where many people don't rush to one another's aid all that often.

People often talk sentimentally or idealistically about compassion. But, crossing over requires denying that very self which we've often protected and maintained. Jesus Christ crossed over to save us (John 3:16). He needed to attend to the needs of a hurting world that mainly snubbed their noses at Him. Imagine Jesus saying: "I saw the headlights of the train of destruction barreling down upon the world. I saw those people in the ditch".

Jesus showed us that the law of love is greater than the law of limits. He crossed the vast gulf between eternity and time. He crossed the vast road between holiness and humanity. He did not stand at the edge of the ditch; horrified, helpless, hurried, or hard. The critical question is…will we be a person who is primarily ruled by a sense of love or by a sense of limits? We don't have to do it. We can accept the limits. It's natural for us to confess our limits and simply pass by on the other side. No human law compels us to cross over to the person in that ditch that we may meet later this week. But if we do—if we choose to move toward the pain of others, rather than around it—we will be walking the way of Jesus. We'll be on the Cross Road to love.

Except for times spent in the comfort and protection of fellow Christians, believers' lives are spent out in the world. This is where our love should shine as we meet and influence those who are searching and struggling to find the Truth of faith. While serving for a couple of years on the staff at the Detroit Rescue Mission, Ernie witnessed men at the very bottom in terms of deadly addictions. Lost and without hope were the men that came there with broken hearts as a last resort. In human terms, they were the viewed as the ungodly. But **"…Christ died for the ungodly"** (Romans 5:6), and this includes each of us. Let each of us point the way to faith in Jesus to others by communicating love to those we come in contact with—the needier the better. Unless God calls you to do so, it is not necessary to travel to foreign lands or to evangelize on urban street corners. Each believer is able to know in her or his heart what God has in mind for them. Where ever it is, and whomever it involves, we communicate the ultimate of faith development by doing it in love.

The receiving of God's precious promises of His divine nature and power are realized in the full development of our faith. Augustine wrote: "Faith is the root and mother of all virtues." The wonderful thing is that faith development not only provides spiritual growth for God's kingdom but it also brings about joy and an exciting, abundant life, here and now—for us and for those we influence. Let our joy shine. Paul Little supported joy so well: "Some people think that God peers over the balcony of heaven trying to find anybody who is enjoying life. And when He spots a happy person, He yells, 'Now cut that out!' That concept of God should make us shudder!"

Where does all this lead? Ignatius, an early church leader, had this to say on the issue relating to Peter's model of faith development: "Out of faith, the root, spring the seven fair fruits of holiness, of which holy love is the fairest and the sweetest." What then is the application of our faith development? It's clear from Scripture that all believers are integral parts of the body of Christ and necessary to the fulfillment of the gospel of love, and this motivates us to move onward and upward on the highway of holiness (Isaiah 35:8, 9) toward our eventual goal of glory and the completion of the mission of the church.

General Douglas MacArthur, on landing in the Philippines on October 20, 1944, was believed to say: "This is the voice of freedom, General MacArthur speaking. People of the Philippines: I have returned. By the grace of almighty God, our forces stand again on Philippine soil ... the hour of your redemption is here ..." MacArthur spoke of the hour of redemption. The people under Japanese captivity were freed by the allied troops' second arrival. It is certainly true that in a dark time in history, the Philippine people were redeemed from the enemy. An end was reached to the heinous death marches and indescribable, inhumane treatment of fellow human beings. Peter (1 Peter 4:7) sounds a similar, yet much more urgent, note of warning and motivation. He wrote, **"The end of all things is near..."** And the writer of the book of Hebrews urges all to come together regularly as children of God (10:25)

...**"not forsaking our own assembling together, as is the habit of some, but encouraging one another; and all the more as you see the day drawing near."** The day refers to the Day of the Lord, when the church body is caught up to be with and to accompany Christ's second coming. Hebrews 10:37 continues with the theme, "For yet in a very little while, He who is coming will come, and He will not delay." John wrote, "Children it is the last hour..." (1 John 2:18). Jesus Himself instructs us in Matthew 24:42, **"Therefore be on the alert, for you do not know which day your Lord is coming."** There is a humorous story of a Scottish lawyer who, because of an accident or misuse, killed another man's horse. Naturally the owner wanted payment plus damages for the loss of the animal. The lawyer acknowledged his liability and willingness to pay, but was short on cash at the moment. He offered his promissory note, which the owner accepted. The lawyer further pressed for the note to bear a date long in the future. "Fix your own date," declared the creditor. The crafty lawyer drew up the note, making it payable on the Day of Judgment. Well, eventually the creditor took the matter to court, and the lawyer in defense asked the judge to look at the note. The judge replied, "The promissory note is perfectly good, sir, and as this is judgment day in this court, I decree that you pay tomorrow."

Because of the fact, the reality, the Truth that the day of redemption is coming, we are told some specific ways to handle our lives while waiting for it. This very practical counsel centers on our ministry to one another. Prayer is a powerful ministry. Ernie recalled the night before he had quadruple bypass surgery that one of the nurses attending him said she had a friend who was a prayer warrior and asked if it would be okay with me to have her pray for you. Of course he said yes, and it gave him a great deal of comfort and spiritual support. The operation took several hours as the surgical team worked over him. Prior to being wheeled into the surgical suite, the lead surgeon assured Ernie that he would do his very best, and would then leave it up to the Lord. Ernie was ready to meet the Lord so there was no fear. God's grace was more than sufficient.

CHAPTER 12

Paul speaks of the power of prayer in Ephesians 6:19 as he addressed the church at Ephesus with these words: **"…and pray on my behalf, that utterance may be given to me in the opening of my mouth, to make known with boldness the mystery of the gospel."**

Also, in Colossians 4:3 he wrote, **"Praying at the same time for us as well, that God will open up to us a door for the word, so that we may speak forth the mystery of Christ."** The great missionary was writing that we should pray for all believers, and in this particular verse, pray for missionaries. These prayers give them boldness and truth when preaching and teaching.

In addition to prayer, Peter speaks of being sober (1 Peter 4:7); the word, sober, in the original Greek means to be self-controlled. This is important counsel. We must be sober and of sound judgment, for these are crucial latter days before Jesus returns. The end is at hand. We see the signs all around us: frequent devastating earthquakes, wars, hatred, terrorism, floods, immorality—the list goes on and on. There is not a limitedness amount of time, and we need to be sober to fulfill our ministry goals. But whether the Lord returns in our lifetime or not, our own day of redemption is near, be it in one minute or one, five, or twenty or more years away. We all will meet our Redeemer soon—one way or another.

Paul, in the discipleship training of his spiritual son, Timothy, urged him to **"...do the work of an evangelist, fulfill your ministry"** (2 Timothy 4:5). Peter's words are for us today. Be sober and fulfill our ministries. Do not delay; our time for doing so is today. Above all, Peter wrote in verse eight, keep fervent in your love for one another, very similar to Paul's words in Colossians 3:14, **"Beyond all these things put on love, which is the perfect bond of unity."**

This is the greatest ministry: love for one another and for the lost and hurting of the world. Love is essential, not optional. It is the summation of Christ's commandment to us (1 John 4:7–8): to love God, and to love one another. And by giving love, it comes right back at us twofold for our wellbeing while on earth. Chuck Swindoll taught: "Without [love], life is a friction-filled series of demands and requirements." Have you noticed this? When our motives for doing things are in love, things just go much smoother. Love is essential for life's fulfillment and enjoyment as God designed it for each of us.

Agape love, therefore, focuses upon affirming strengths in one another rather than criticizing weaknesses. We all have weaknesses, heaven knows. But love is commitment. Love is listening and encouraging when others are hurting, even if we are hurting ourselves at the time—which will most probably be the case. We need to be sensitive and not stingy in the sharing of our love.

The writer of Hebrews 13:1 states: **"Let love of the brethren continue. Do not neglect to show hospitality to strangers, for by this some have entertained angels without knowing it."**

This is a great reason to show hospitality. Opening homes and offices for visitors, meals for those unable to do so for themselves, helping young mothers with their small children in time of need or when the parents just need a weekend or day away, giving people car rides when they can't get to the doctor or church or the store—you can fill in the blanks. Much goes on behind the scenes, but God knows what happens and when sharing occurs.

Peter's concern and teaching here are both clear and practical. We are to minister (that is, serve) one another, as each one has received a special gift or gifts to do so effectively (1 Peter 4:10). The word gift here in verse ten is translated in the Greek as *charisma*; it denotes a very special kind of gift. It comes from a root word meaning grace. Peter is writing about grace-gifts or spiritual gifts that come from Holy Spirit. Do you know your gift or gifts? The Apostle Paul teaches that there are various gifts and varieties of ministries, but to each Christian is given the manifestation of the Spirit for the common good (1 Corinthians 12). These gifts are to be distinguished from natural talents, which have been given to all at the time of physical birth. Spiritual gifts are given to all believers according to the will of Holy Spirit at one's spiritual new birth.

What is the purpose of these gifts? How should they be used? Employ them! This is the action verb involved. Don't hide them; we use them to serve one another. In His parable on gifts in Luke 19:13, Jesus spoke of workers using their gifts until He comes back.

Peter lists two practical ways to employ our gifts. First, in verse eleven, **"Whoever speaks, is to do so as one who is speaking the utterances of God"** (1 Peter 4:11). This does not refer only to teachers and preachers, but to all. We are told in Ephesians 4:29, **"Let no unwholesome word proceed from your mouth, but only such a word as is good for edification according to the need of the moment, so that it will give grace to those who hear."**

A second example is in the power of our serving one another, **"Whoever serves is to do so as one who is serving by the strength which God supplies." The Bible refers to all believers when referring to ministering priests, not just an elect hierarchy. "You all also, as living stones, are being built up as a spiritual house for a holy priesthood"** (1 Peter 2:5, 9).

King David spoke to his assembly, and his words speak to us and to our local assemblies. The words are found in 1 Chronicles (29:11–13).

> **"Yours, O Lord, is the greatest and the power and the glory and the victory and the majesty, indeed everything that is in the heavens and the earth: Yours is the dominion, O Lord, and you exalt Yourself as head over all. Both**

riches and honor come from You, and You rule over all, and in Your hand is power and might; and it lies in Your hand to make great, and to strengthen everyone. Now therefore our God, we thank You, and praise Your glorious name."

CHAPTER 13

Traveling over the Mackinac Bridge that spans the upper and lower peninsulas of Michigan, Ernie once again recollected boyhood experiences. From the crest of the bridge, the Grand Hotel of Mackinac Island with its gleaming white porch could be seen in the distance; the longest summer hotel porch in the world. Horses and buggies await passengers departing from the ferries that ply the Straits of Mackinac between St. Ignace or Mackinaw City and the island loading docks. Grand Hotel hansom carriages transport visitors to the hotel. Various other horse drawn cabs are destined for the other hotels and tourist homes. The only motor-driven vehicles allowed on the Island, even during the tourist season to this day, are the fire and medical emergency trucks. So the island is a bustle of bicycles and horse-drawn buggies of one type or another.

The story of the bridge's founding is a wonder in itself. Prentiss M. Brown, a former US senator hailing from the Upper Peninsula was a master of persuasion. He was able to convince his colleagues in Congress to approve the construction of one of the longest bridges in the nation—one that many believed could not be built in the turbulent waters connecting Lake Huron and Lake Michigan. Not only was the project one of questionable possibility but it was also of dubious economic value.

Senator Brown proposed a bridge to be constructed between Mackinaw City and St. Ignace, two small towns of several hundred people each. But there was a statewide need to connect the two peninsulas, and Congress, as well as Wall Street, was convinced. Investment bankers underwrote the venture, and the rest is history. A marvel of modern civil engineering is now a well-traveled and financial success.

But this crossing brought to mind a much younger Ernest B. de Beaubien, dredging up earlier boyhood memories of long ago when Ernie was on a camping trip to the Upper Peninsula. He and his camper buddies were loaded in the back of the Camp Hayo-Went-Ha truck along with duffle bags filled with sleeping bags and who knows what else, as well as boxes of provisions for a week in the wilderness. As the truck crossed the bridge in a car ferry and then cruised along highway US 2 into the city of Escanaba, Ernie had the clear vision that someday he would live in the Upper Peninsula. This is the land of Hiawatha and the Indian maiden, Pocahontas that Rudyard Kipling wrote about. The scene unveiled itself again with beautiful vistas of white pine, birch, and sparkling lakes great and small. Lake Michigan is on the southern shore, with endless waves washing up clean white sand to form majestic dunes.

The destination of the camping trip was the Porcupine Mountains State Park located in the northwestern region of the Peninsula. This district, adjoining the majestic Lake Superior, is notable for many things. It is the western border of an area once bustling with copper mines and hordes of all sorts of folk with the ambition or greed that accompanies mining booms. Copper was king from the village of White Pine to the northern end of the Keweenaw Peninsula where everyone was in search of the precious metal. The rush rivaled the more-documented '49ers Gold Rush of California.

In addition to copper barons from Boston and other areas of the east came the lumberjacks and logging entrepreneurs. Millions of acres of virgin white pine forest along with statuesque stands of oak brought wealth or famine to the woodsmen. The romance of this extraordinary land was attractive to Ernie, and he somehow believed he would be a part of it all one day. Central to the copper economy was the Michigan College of Mines in Houghton that turned out the mining engineers for the copper boom, as well as the iron ore mines of the central Upper Peninsula surrounding Marquette County.

So, continuing across the Mackinac Bridge, dubbed the Big Mac, Ernie's thoughts returned to the reality of the more recent past. Indeed, as he had returned earlier in his adult life to raise his daughters in an environment of horses, dogs, cats, ducks, and mountains of winter snow. Winter winds travel over the Big Lake, bringing in monstrous Alberta Clipper storms that dump snow squalls on the lee side of Lake Superior. While more populated regions such as Western New York State receive more weather coverage by the media, the Keweenaw snowfall far exceeds the more published places. In fact, there is routinely more snow in the Keweenaw than anywhere else east of the Rocky Mountains.

The copper and lumber barons have long since gone, taking their fortunes with them, leaving a depressed region in their wake. Yet, the "Yoopers" (for "UPers"), are the hardy folk of the Upper Peninsula, who would have it no other way. The copper and lumber booms brought in resilient immigrants from Finland, England, Italy, and elsewhere, including French Canadians who intermingled with the native Ojibwa Indians. These diverse persons brought a culture of independence and strength of character that survived the post-copper era. The Michigan College of Mines later became the Michigan Technological University, and is today one of the leading higher education institutions of America.

Another local icon was the Detroit and Northern Savings and Loan. This banking institution was developed in Hancock, the twin city across the Portage Canal from Houghton and the home of Michigan Tech. The firm expanded, under the leadership and vision of the Seaton family of Hancock, from the Keweenaw Peninsula to the Detroit metropolitan area. Over time, and to the changing climate of banks and mortgage markets in general, savings and loans began to merge for the economic advantage of mass.

There is a culture at MTU, similar to most universities, which finds expression in the dichotomy of administration and academic faculty. A clear example of this tension took place in a situation that included the storied financial interests apart from forest products and copper mining. There occurred at the time at Michigan Technological University an ill-founded enterprise dubbed the 'Ventures Group' whose mission was to transfer local research to market application. The notion was good, but greed in some of the administration officials brought its demise. Enter Steven P. Dresch, dean of the business school at MTU. An investigative reporter at heart, Dr. Dresch led a crusade to uncover the scoundrels in the enterprise group. Eventually two officials received prison experiences. Driesch went on to become a state representative in the Michigan legislature in Lansing, and after his term ended he took up investigative assignments full time. The dangers involved in investigative reporting didn't kill him, but smoking later did.

The university's leadership and faculty are currently on higher ground, and many of the smartest and the best students continue to enroll. Students matriculate from hundreds of miles away to traipse through the snow and hard winters on the way to receiving a world-class engineering or science education. Forestry, business, humanities, and social sciences round out a student's undergraduate and graduate degree program options, producing finished products sought after by leading firms of the region, and indeed the nation and the world.

Global demand for MTU graduates is now a two-way street. Many of the academically gifted and financially well-placed students of Asia are numbered in the large percentage of international scholars pursuing graduate degrees at Tech. They can be seen cruising the campus in their upscale Japanese automobiles. This, along with the large population of European emigrants, has given the UP a marvelous mix of cultures. It is indeed, as witnessed by Ernie, a small, foreign-mission field right at his front door. Ernie loves to share the Truth of eternal life through Jesus Christ in the wonderful country churches he associated himself with, and in personal relationships with students from China and India and other countries of Asia.

CHAPTER 14

It was a very long stretch of time from the sunshine of youth—seemingly endless prisms of hope and wonderment of life—to the present moment of Ernest B. de Beaubien's life. He found himself often engrossed in thought as he reflected on the myriad changes taking place during his lifetime. Where had the time gone? But he was now ready to travel upward to his true home in glory, to be with his Lord Jesus and other departed loved ones. He is at complete peace, having found and embraced the Truth of life in God's Word and also knowing true love with his wife, Lorna. The world, however, is not at peace. Much of the world's teeming population is endlessly hurrying here and there in a frenzied rush to nowhere. Most everything now is judged on the basis of speed. Instant gratification is the mantra. Humanity, as it existed since the dawn of history, is sliding down the slippery slope to technological singularity; the god of technology is replacing the one true God in the minds of the lost as the fountainhead of knowledge. Super computers match—and, according to techno-futurists, soon may exceed—the intelligence of the human brain in computational knowledge and may become mimes of human characteristics. At the rate of current technological development, it is speculated by the hyper-futurists that a machine will, in the relatively near future, surpass all human stored knowledge.

The devotees of strong artificial intelligence (AI) do not look upon machine understanding as the ultimate attack on the fabric of human history. Yet radical singularity poses a pseudo-threat to the sacred meaning of eternal life, with its alternative electronic eternity. The failure to recognize the sacredness and uniqueness of the human soul and spirit has precipitated a headlong pursuit for the electronic replacement of biological existence. The search for the fountain of youth is taking a radical turn, yet is thought by many to be technologically plausible. The gist of the faulty concept of technological perpetual existence fails to take into account that eternal life is already available through God's plan of salvation. Life is spiritual, the physical body merely a vehicle for the spark of life. However, the technological futurists are promoting a techno-doctrine that involves an electronic 'rapture.' The claim is that while the body may die, the essence of 'personhood' is encapsulated through connectivity with the electronic 'savior' for ongoing electronic life.

The Truth relating to the final events of the old order of time and occurrences was opening visions right before Ernie's eyes as his physical life. Latter-day events ae occurring precisely as God designed. Starting with the reestablishment of Israel as a nation in 1948 and, more recently, plans for the rebuilding of the Jewish temple in Jerusalem; the door is opening for the apostasy (antichrist) to appear and desecrate the name of God. Transitory world peace commences with the advent of globalization of political, economic, religious, and social domains. Ever since the beginning of the new millennium global unification has been a quest, fascination, and focus of development in the centers of power and influence. The world more and more embraces global ecumenical singularity. With this, fundamentalists in the major religions, other than authentic Christianity, coexist in a fragile peace leading up to the years of the Great Tribulation prophesized by Christ (Matthew 24) and various other Bible authors.

The Day of the Lord, as foretold by the Apostle Paul, consists of the 'catching up' of Jesus' redeemed, dead and alive, in the air to be with Him, and to escort Him back to Earth. Many theologians refer to this event as the rapture, but that word is not found in most versions of the Bible. The Latin Vulgate version has it as *rapere*, meaning to seize, translated in English as rapture. These events (the catching up of the redeemed and the second coming of Christ) take place as a lengthy occurrence commencing just before or just after the rebuilding of the Jewish temple and the coming of the apostasy (1 Thessalonians 4:16, 17; 2 Thessalonians 2:1, 3).

Christians are being bombarded with end times prophecy both from print and electronic channels. It is more and more evident that the process of final history is moving forward rapidly according to God's plan. After the renewal of the Israeli state in 1948, many natural events occurred in more recent years. The next event of major importance could be the rebuilding of the Jewish temple in Jerusalem. Knowledgeable researchers claim that the architectural plans for the temple are already completed and workers are starting to be hired for its construction. The timing of these developments is not to be known. No one is able to confirm the timing, as the plan relating to the Day of the Lord is clearly and most definitely in God's hands.

Paul states in 2 Thessalonians 2:3–4 that the man of lawlessness "…**takes his seat in the temple of God, displaying himself as being God."**

The date and time of that glorious day is unknown, and those that attempt to determine it teach falsely and will be judged for doing so. However, God has provided a general overview of the occurrence. Scripture in this regard, as in most passages in the Bible, can be defined in different ways; godly men and women differ on the time and epochs of the Day of the Lord and the accompanying catching up of the saints to meet the Lord on His second coming. Some folks are pre-tribulation teachers, separating the gathering together and Christ's coming as two separate occurrences. Others take a different approach to Scripture. It is always a good practice in the interpretation of any passage of God's Word to take the clearest path to the meaning. We may turn to 1 Thessalonians 5:1–2:

> **"Now as to the times and the epochs, brethren, you have no need of anything to be written to you. For you yourselves know full well that the Day of the Lord will come just like a thief in the night."**

A further interpretation of this passage about the Day of the Lord is that it is one continuous event. Some interpret it as being two separate events: the gathering up of the saints, as Paul states in 1 Thessalonians 4:13–18, and then seven years later the coming of the Lord. A thesis can be advanced for the day as being one event with two parts: the gathering together of the saints and the triumphant return of Christ along with His own and the heavenly host of angels.

While the exact timing is unknown to humans, the Day of the Lord is fast approaching. The smart computer, in the control of Antichrist, would be all that is necessary for the final battle between good and evil. It is speculated by various techno-prophets that in the near future, implanted devices or chips such as a mark on the hand or forehead (Revelation 13:15) might interconnect directly with the human brain. A neural-electronic splicing would play directly into the hands of a global despot set on identifying and persecuting those following the one true God. Persecution of Christ's truly redeemed would simply involve the compilation of a database through a search by the ultimate expert system: the *singularity* mind.

Revelation 13 provides a conceivable scenario whereby Satan gives the dragon (antichrist) his power. The dragon is empowered by another beast (electronic singularity); this electronic false prophet would be Antichrist's enforcer, identifying with instantaneous technological speed all of humanity refusing to worship Satan. Signs and wonders could also be performed through a superhuman mind. Satan (spirit), Antichrist (man), and Singularity (machine) would then take on the personification of an unholy trinity.

Ernie's belief in the Truth takes on aspects surrounding the important event to face humankind in the future: the second coming of our Lord Jesus Christ. The times and events of the world speak on the urgency that cannot be dismissed from our minds.

CHAPTER 15

A Kentucky weather forecast omitted the word "showers," and the forecaster said, "There is less than five percent chance of tonight and tomorrow." With the events moving so rapidly toward the fulfillment of Bible prophecy, this Kentucky forecast sounds alarmingly accurate. Someone once said that prophecy is history of the future. This is certainly true of biblical prophecy. God is completely truthful and one hundred percent correct in all He communicates to us about what will happen, and this will continue to be the case until the fulfillment of all prophecy provided us within the canon of Scripture.

We are able to set the foundation for Christ's Second Advent: First, the promise of the second advent of Christ, and second, God's agenda for this most important future event. Verse one of 2 Thessalonians chapter two provides the promise right at the start, the promise of the coming. Second coming theology clearly should be at the very heart of every Christian believer's faith and hope. The very magnitude of verses in the Bible that

God devotes to this subject is proof enough of the importance He places on our knowledge and understanding of the event.

I'd like to share some revealing facts provided by John MacArthur in his book *The Second Coming of the Lord Jesus Christ*. "Perhaps a third or more of the prophetic passages [in the Bible] refer to the Second Coming of Christ or events related to it. It is a major theme of both Old Testament and New Testament prophecy." MacArthur goes on to provide specifics.

"The entire Old Testament is filled with prophecies of the coming Deliverer—at least 333 distinct promises by one count. More than a hundred of those prophecies were literally fulfilled at the first advent of Christ…it stands to reason, then, that the remaining two-thirds of Old Testament prophecies will also be fulfilled literally. And that requires the return of Jesus Christ to this Earth."

Something God believes so important certainly demands more than our casual interest and cursory knowledge. Much time is spent in study and worship of Christ's first advent, and most rightly so. There is a need to equally understand the second coming theology in order to apply this knowledge to the planning of our lives. Ernie recalls little else his mother shared with him at a very early age other than the second coming of Christ. He remembers sitting on his mother's lap and hearing that Jesus will be coming back. It may have been at the time of Christmas and the Lord's first advent.

Vine's *Expository Dictionary* defines the Greek word *parousia* for coming as used in this context, literally denoting both an arrival and a consequent presence with. *Parousia* future coming events: the gathering together (catching up) with Him of all believers (1 Thessalonians 4:17). The coming signifies not merely His momentary coming for His saints, but His presence with them from that moment until His manifestation to the world at large and for evermore.

As to the chronology relating to the Day of the Lord, Paul speaks clearly in 2 Thessalonians 2 about three things: (1) certainty of the coming, (2) the chronology of events, and (3) the implications for our life due to Christ's coming. In addition to the above Scripture God devoted to the second coming theology, the truth is reinforced with just a few of the additional references where the Greek word *parousia* is used.

Paul preached hope to the church at Corinth about Jesus' resurrection and our gathering to Him at the time of His coming. **"Christ the first fruits, after that those who are Christ's at His coming"** (1 Corinthians 15:23). Luke writes that the two angels at Christ's ascent into Heaven on the cloud promised **"This Jesus, who has been taken up from you into heaven, will come in just the same way as you have watched Him go into heaven"** (Acts 1:11). Our Lord Himself had the following to say, **"For the Son of Man is going to come in the glory of His Father with His angels; and will then recompense every man according to his deeds"** (Matthew 16:27).

Matthew 24 is devoted to the details of this coming. Verse twenty-seven declares, **"For just as the lightning comes from the east, and flashes even to the west, so shall the coming of the Son of Man be."** Second Peter 1:16: **"We made known to you the power and coming of our Lord Jesus Christ."** We have also Jesus' comforting words in John 14:1–4, **"Let not your heart be troubled; believe in God, believe also in Me.**

In My Father's house are many dwelling places; if it were not so, I would have told you; for I go to prepare a place for you. And if I go and prepare a place for you, I will come again, and receive you to myself; that where I am, there you may be also." Praise God!

There is a crucial doctrinal development needing to be addressed at this point, for it impacts all further study of this whole passage. There are two phrases in Second Thessalonians relating to the second coming. The first concerns the coming, and the second is our gathering together to Him. Paul teaches that the coming of our Lord Jesus Christ and our gathering together to Him are stated in chapter 2, verse three,

> **"Let no one in any way deceive you, for it [or *that day* in some versions] will not come unless the apostasy comes first."**

A singular event is assumed. He had taught about this in depth during his previous stay in Thessalonica. He taught the believers about the circumstances surrounding the event, and reminds them of this in verse five. Both of the phrases—the coming of the Lord and our gathering together to Him—are tied together.

While it is one event, it could be interpreted as an elongated event shaped as an upside-down letter U: The gathering together with Him of all believers at the catching up to be with Christ coming in the clouds but not completely to Earth; the seven years gathering of saints and the heavenly host; then His coming to Earth at the last battle with the Devil and his cohorts at Armageddon. This is emphasized in 1 Thessalonians 4:16–18, which promises that

> "...the Lord Himself will descend from heaven with a shout with the archangel, and with the trumpet of God; and the dead in Christ shall rise first. Then we who are alive and remain shall be caught up together with them in the clouds to meet the Lord in the air, and thus we shall always be with the Lord. Therefore comfort one another with these words."

J. N. Darby of the Plymouth Brethren introduced a novel idea around 1830 that these two phrases refer to two completely different events. Thus there came into being for the first time in the history of the church the interpretative scheme that there will be a "gathering together with Him" occurring at some time before Christ's coming. As stated above, Paul connects the two events as one. He expressed this idea as he said, "let no one in any way deceive you, for *it* [or *that day*] will not come" until two future events occur, which he identified as the apostasy and the appearance of the man of lawlessness. With this interpretation, it is difficult to suppose that the "day of the Lord" in verse two belongs in a different time from that in view in 1 Thessalonians 4:13–18. However, the two could very well be, one continuous event over time. In other words, the 'rapture' could take place immediately, or around the time of the rebuilding of the Jewish temple.

Apparently at the time of Paul's writing certain persons had misinformed the believers at Thessalonica by way of false teaching or even with letters supposedly from Paul that were counterfeits. Paul says in verse two that these perhaps were letters as if from me. The contents of these false teachings regarding the coming of the Lord are not shared with his readers. We are not told many things, yet we are assured from these and supporting Scripture passages three things: Jesus Christ will return, that all believers in Him (dead and alive) will be caught up to accompany Him to Earth, and that we should not be shaken in our faith by false teaching. Our complete faith can rest on these assurances. Let us cling to the promise that He's coming back!

He's Coming Back

I see the world so differently
Since I accepted Jesus
The heartaches come
But now, I'm not destroyed

When I look all around me
At the anger and the sadness
There's something
That can fill my heart with joy

He's coming—He's coming back
We need to tell the whole world that
And let them know that Jesus is the way
He's coming back in great majesty
To take us home eternally
We ought to live as though it were today

Our Lord never intended
For us to feel at home here
We're citizens of heaven, you and me

Whenever I'm discouraged
I think of Christ returning
And what a day of glory that will be

Faye La Beau © 1982

CHAPTER 16

Obviously an event of this magnitude to the world—and to us individually—needs to be maintained by faith in our hearts and minds and looked at in depth to completely understand and to plan for. Paul and his colleagues, who knew more about their converts' problem than we today can know, judged that it would help them to be told something about the sequence of events leading up to the day of the Lord. Therefore, the chronology is helpful to strengthen and maintain our faith as well.

We are told clearly in verse three that the complete coming of the Lord will not come unless the apostasy (or rebellion) comes first and that the man of lawlessness, the son of destruction, is revealed. Jesus, in His chronology of the day of the Lord in Matthew 24, states the same thoughts as Paul as He teaches that "when you see the abomination of destruction which was spoken of through Daniel the prophet, standing in the holy place … there will be a great tribulation, such as has not occurred since the beginning of the world until now, nor ever shall" (verses 15 and 21). The signs of His coming are spelled out for us in Matthew 24:29–31.

> **"But immediately after the tribulation of those days the sun will be darkened, and the moon will not give its light, and the stars will fall from the sky, and the powers of the heavens will be shaken, and then the sign of the Son of Man will appear in the sky, and then all tribes of the earth will mourn, and they will see the Son of Man coming on the clouds of the sky with power and great glory. And He will send forth His angels with a great trumpet and they will gather together His elect from the four winds [already in heaven], from one end of the sky to the other."**

The word for apostasy or rebellion spoken of in 2 Thessalonians 2:3 denotes either political rebellion, as written by the Jewish historian, Josephus, concerning the Jewish revolt against Rome, or religious defection, as in Acts 21:21, the abandonment of Moses' Law. Since the reference here is to a worldwide rebellion against divine authority at the end of the age, the ideas of political and religious apostasy are in some manner combined.

The leader of the apostasy is described by two phrases and characterized by his opposition to the divine law and therefore he is doomed to destruction. The idea that he is to be revealed implies that the man of lawlessness, like the Lord Jesus, is to have his own coming, and will in some sense be a rival, but false, messiah. This seems to be in line with John's teaching of the Antichrist coming (1 John 2:18). We know that the son of destruction is empowered by Satan, further proof that this individual is the Antichrist spoken of by John. He has all the power and signs and false wonders that Satan can provide him. In Revelation 13, John more graphically describes this energizing with all power, as well as other signs of falsehood in the Antichrist. Apparently Satan will restore the Antichrist to life in imitation of the resurrection of Christ.

This passage in 2 Thessalonians is difficult, and made more so by verses six and seven. Paul talks about a restrainer of the man of lawlessness, but is very vague as to who or what this restrainer is. In the long and complex history of the interpretations of this passage, every possible alternative to the identification of this restraining force or person has been suggested. Perhaps the most honest and frank view of this passage about the restrainer was put forth by Augustine in the fifth century (*The City of God*, chapter 20): "I admit that the meaning of the [restrainer] completely escapes me."

What is important is that the doctrine of the *parousia* become established and settled in our faith and a source of comfort and strength. We may wish that Paul had been clearer about the apostasy, the man of sin, and the restrainer. But he moves quickly to a description of the future, that day when God's final word will be spoken in the coming of Jesus Christ. In every way the lawless one, the man of sin and son of perdition, is portrayed as a counterfeit Christ. He professes to be God. He works with all power, signs, and lying wonders. But he will be defeated and destroyed by Christ Himself. Verse eight is very clear.

> **"The Lord will slay him with the breath of His mouth and bring to an end by the appearance of His coming."**

The Lord is returning, and each of us who professes faith in Jesus will be caught up to meet Him and abide with Him, apart from the great tribulation on earth, putting an end to the power and presence of Satan and evil. We know Christ is coming. Although we do not know the day and time, we know the framework. We have the promise. We also know that current world point to the need for preparation for the greatest event of all time. Cling to the Promise! This time in history is the most exciting and hopeful or the most disturbing and fearful, depending on where we stand with the Lord. The coming triumphal return of Christ has unavoidable consequences for every person on Earth—both those who accept Christ as Lord and for those who don't.

Let us turn our attention now to the relevance of Christ's coming for unbelievers and believers.

Throughout this narrative of Ernie's pilgrimage we have explored the promise and God's agenda for our communication with Him because of Christ's first advent. It is only appropriate to conclude the study with a focus on Christ's second coming to Earth. The promise is clear: 2 Thessalonians 2:1 declares that our Lord Jesus Christ will come again and will gather all believers in Him to Himself. Verse eight promises that the Lord will then slay Antichrist and bring about the end of Satan's reign of evil upon the earth. Paul speaks with clarity about urgent implications for every human soul related to this second coming. Let us pick up the text at this point in 2 Thessalonians 2:10–17.

What if we are indeed living in the last days on this earth? Evidence points to this conclusion. If so, this is bound to bring a certain reality to our thinking and faith. This is not a storybook tale. This is a truth found in the inerrant Word of God. Jesus will be returning. Some of you may be skeptical as you read this statement. There were skeptics in biblical times and there are skeptics now. But Peter has the answer for skeptics. It is important to read from Peter's second letter, as it is relevant to the text of 2 Thessalonians.

A paraphrase of 2 Peter 3:3 and following tells us that in the last days mockers will come with their mocking, following after their own lusts, and saying:

> **"Where is the promise of His coming? You Christians have been talking about that for two thousand years, and all continues just the same."**

> But Peter continues, **"Do not let this one fact escape you, beloved, that with the Lord one day is as a thousand years, and a thousand years as one day. The Lord is not slow about His promise, as some count slowness, but is**

patient toward you, not wishing for any to perish, but for all to come to repentance."

The day of the Lord will come like a thief, and we ought to be holy in our conduct and godliness, looking for the hastening of the coming of the day of God.

The Lord wants everyone on planet Earth to hear the gospel, to have a chance at accepting Truth before the end comes. And you know the end could be soon. We do not know the day or hour. Paul tells us to watch for the signs. The signs we are seeing in the world point toward a rapid approach to the coming of Christ. Technology is already in place to reach virtually every corner of the earth, including the hidden peoples. Reliable estimations are that the entire world population will be able to hear the good news in a language they understand.

As we progress through this third millennium after Christ's first advent, significant things are happening around us. Gigantic plans of evangelism on a global scale are being creatively conceived and will be executed by many different groups within the body of Christ. It is significant that most of these movements commenced in AD 2000, the target year for an unprecedented worldwide harvest for the kingdom. If only one or two of these strategic plans fully succeed in their missions, the world will truly be turned upside down. A few of these movements can be used as examples.

Bold Mission Thrust is the Southern Baptist strategy for world evangelization. The Bold Mission Thrust is a massive movement involving scores of agencies, thousands of churches, and millions of church members around the world. The objective is to enable every person in the world to hear and respond to the gospel of Christ. The North American Congress on the Holy Spirit and World Evangelization has been attended by many thousands of Christians in the charismatic movement. A strategy was set in place to preach the gospel to all nations.

The Roman Catholics planned a one-billion-dollar project called Evangelization 2000. The project was to give Jesus Christ more believers than not (nonbelievers) in the world.

The US Center for World Mission is working a plan to chart the course of a cooperative mission effort. Their belief is that there are ample evangelical resources in the world community to make a serious attempt to plant churches within every people group. They believe that the task is more readily within our grasp than ever before in history, and that the very end of history may therefore be near.

There are many more movements leading to the evangelization of the world; the list of strategies is impressive. The popular culture, as expressed through Hollywood projects, become involved several years ago through Mel Gibson's *The Passion of the Christ*, as seen by millions worldwide. Separate from traditional secular Hollywood is an evangelistic movement also within the entertainment industry. A leader in the movement is *PureFlix*, a streaming platform devoted exclusively to faith and values based programming. Some evangelistic programs are still in the embryonic stage pending further development, such as the International Satellite Mission of the Billy Graham Evangelistic Association. Some are just beginning, such as the book distribution plan of the World Literature Crusade that puts two books on salvation and Christian growth in the hands of every home on earth in their own language.

CHAPTER 17

What is God trying to tell us today? Are we listening with any discernment to the remarkable events taking place in Europe, Russia, China, and Latin America? While freedom to worship and to witness is increasingly dangerous in communist countries, there is an underground explosion of Christ conversions now in previously closed regions. End times development in the Holy Land and the war against evil commencing after the September 9, 2001 (9/11) tragedy are escalating events.

The earth's history is winding down. The dropping of the watershed is leading to conditions for a devastating drought; population explosions are becoming unbearable for the amount of productive land; the amounts of earthquakes appear in great numbers and seem to be increasing rapidly. The widespread plague (AIDS) that attacks immunity systems reached many societal groups. More recently in the 21st century, an even more widespread devastation became worldwide in new outbreaks of deadly viruses such as the Covid-19 pandemic, killing millions worldwide. These occurrences, and many more, are coming to a critical head at this time. The events occurring today along with the technology and strategies to evangelize the world need to grab the attention of every thinking man and woman.

And the world is being prepared for the antichrist. Devil worship is closing in on all sides, and the camps are lining up. The polarization of Christians and those that will follow the antichrist is widening and becoming clearly defined. No longer can we be in both camps with one foot in each. Take a look at the bookstores or the Internet. If you have not visited the religion section of a major bookstore or online vendor of books, it is an eye-opener. New Age materials are rampant, taking up most of the shelf or website space, leaving only a smaller section for biblical materials.

The time is right to put our lives in line with Christ's coming and His judgments. Jesus made a very clear statement to everyone when He said **"for the Son of Man is going to come in the glory of His Father with His angels; and will then recompense every man according to His deeds"** (Matthew 16:27). Every person will be recompensed. There's good and bad news related to this statement. First the bad news—but written with love.

God is sovereign even in the activities of the powers of evil. The result will be that many men and woman will believe what is false, as Satan works through the antichrist. It is not the elect that are being led astray in the present context, but those who are on the way to perdition, those whose unbelief has made them gullible. Verse eleven speaks of a power being set in operation with the unbeliever at the time of antichrist that makes them prone to embrace error or be led astray. The true

God is not the author of this infatuation; it is as Paul puts it in (2 Corinthians 4:4), **"...the god of this world has blinded the minds of the unbelieving, that they might not see the light of the gospel of the glory of Christ."** Paul wrote earlier in the passage that certain developments precede the day of the Lord. These events are sinister enough. They will involve a widespread rebellion against God, led by the one who is the very embodiment of lawlessness, the one who will try to usurp the throne of God and claim divine honors for himself.

But nothing is as fearsome as the wrath of the Lord. It is detailed for all to read in Revelation 19:11–21. The Word of God, mounted on a white horse, smites His enemies with the sharp sword proceeding from His mouth and throws the "beast" (corresponding to the man of lawlessness [Antichrist]), his agent (the false prophet), and those who worshipped the beast into the lake of fire and brimstone. So great will be the slaughter in the war of Armageddon that an angel will call together the birds of mid-heaven to eat the flesh of those who fall in battle. Although a great deal of physical life will be destroyed, the souls of the unbelieving live on and will be judged during the great white throne judgment to follow. And although Satan will be imprisoned, the evil one will not be damned to the lake of fire until just before the great white throne judgment. Even then the devil will not die, but will be tormented day and night forever and ever (Revelation 20:10). And anyone's name not in the Lamb's Book of Life will also experience the second death of the lake of fire (20:15).

Now Ernie turns to the good news. Scripture is just as plain for believers, but the message is one of great hope and thanksgiving, not darkness and hopelessness. Paul had earlier given assurance in his first letter to the Thessalonians. We as believers are not in darkness (i.e., we are not in the state of separation from God as are unbelieves), and that last day will not overtake us like a thief. We, like those believers at Thessalonica, are told what to expect preceding Christ's coming so that we can prepare. All who believe are of light and the day, not of night or darkness. Verse 11 is clear as to what we must now do (cf. 1 Thessalonians 5:11).

Whether Ernie's or any other believer's body dies before Christ's return or is still alive on Earth at the time, all will live together always with Him. What are we to do for the short time we have left?

There is a great ministry for each of us in these last days to do what Paul urges: "[to] encourage one another, and to build up one another."

This is what the Word of God tells us we must do as believing brothers and sisters. We need to support others. Seek out a few who you can trust. We need others for encouragement and accountability. This Christian fellowship really works!

Have those in our families had an opportunity to hear the gospel? How about our next-door neighbor? Work associates? Is Christ really Lord over every area of your life? Christ is returning. Let's live as if it were today. It is impossible to take Jesus and the Bible seriously without taking in this Truth. To view history as being without meaning, ending either in a whimper or a bang, is contradictory to Scripture. And it is also contradictory to view history as gradually progressing through human effort to universal and enduring peace and love. The biblical view of history always points to the day of the Lord. Consistently, Paul concludes his teaching sections on this subject with an admonition to use the doctrine to comfort one another, to edify and build up the church, and to strengthen our resolve to be faithful in our service to Christ through our love to one another.

The choice is ours to make this very day, this very moment. The ultimate Truth in the Scriptures cannot be ignored. This is no time to procrastinate if you have not accepted Christ. Perhaps there will not be another time. For those of us who are in Christ this is a time of hope, and we need to share this hope with others. There are many who dispel the Truth that salvation comes only one way…through Christ. We've been hearing a great deal these days that Christianity as not the one true way to God. Let's take a look at the Truth.

Matthew 7:13-14 reads as follows. **"Enter by the narrow gate, for the gate is wide and the way is broad that leads to destruction, and many are those who enter by it. For the gate is small and the way is narrow that leads to life, and few are those who find it."**

The gate leading to the Kingdom of Heaven is synonymous with life; destruction relates to being in eternal hell and separated from God. Jesus' allegory in Matthew is similar to that in Luke but in Luke's gospel it points to a narrow door rather than a gate. Luke chapter 13 verse 24 reads:

> "Strive to enter by the narrow door; for many, I tell you, will seek to enter and will not be able."

There are any number of paths to arrive at the narrow door or gate, but only one way to enter, and that is to follow the Great Shepherd, Jesus Christ as personal savior. The Palestinian shepherds of old led their sheep; they did not drive them. The sheep followed because they knew the shepherd's voice and trusted him. The sheep court was surrounded by walls but open to the sky and had only one entrance. The walls kept the sheep from wandering and protected them from wild animals. Similarly, we have the choice to follow Christ the Great Shepherd; God does not force us to accept His gift of grace. But, if we do, we are able to enter the one and only door to eternal life with God and are forever protected. In John chapter 10 verse 1, 7, and 9 we read Jesus' words:

> **"Truly, truly, I say to you, he who does not enter by the door into the fold of the sheep, but climbs up some other way, he is a thief and a robber…Truly, truly I say to you, I am the door of the sheep…if anyone enters through Me, he will be saved…"** Jesus often surprised people with teachings that cut across the grain of human nature. **"Lose your life to save it." "Pray for your enemies." "Turn the other cheek."**

These, and many others, are revolutionary teachings that Jesus gave. But, by far, the most radical assertion that Jesus ever uttered is in the fourteenth chapter of John, in the sixth verse,

> "I am the way and the truth and the life. No
> one comes to the Father but through me."

This claim rankles many people like nothing else. Those persons advocating a global religion (which includes many of our political leaders, the liberal media, and even more and more so-called Christians) call this belief narrow-minded. It's been called bigoted. It's been called snobbish. But we are not surprised, as we are told animosity toward Christians will occur in the last days. Perhaps some of you agree, and something inside of you chafes at the idea that Jesus is the only way to God; for we are living in a world where there seems to be endless options in virtually every area of life. But Jesus declared:

> "I am the way, and the truth, and the life: no
> one comes to the Father but through Me."

Jesus was telling the Truth when he uttered those words. I believe he said those words not out of arrogance, but out of great compassion. When you look closer at it, this statement by Jesus makes ultimate sense.

Why is this claim so controversial? One reason is that it strikes at the core of three great myths about religion. The first myth about religion is that all religions are basically the same. You've probably heard people say through the years that there may be surface-level distinctions between various world religions but that there are many paths to God? If you strip them down to their essentials, all religions fundamentally teach the same thing. In other words, all spiritual paths lead up the same mountain because all religions basically teach the brotherhood and the sisterhood of men and women and the universal fatherhood of God. Let's concede that there is some common ground shared by many of the world's religions, especially when you look at the level of basic values and statements of belief about morality.

However, the matchlessness of Christianity is rooted in the uniqueness of Jesus himself. For instance, other religious leaders say, "Follow me and I'll show you how to find the truth." But Jesus says, **"I am the truth."** Other religious leaders say, "Follow me and I'll show you the way to salvation." But Jesus says, **"I am the way to eternal life."** Other religious leaders say, "Follow me and I'll show you how you can become enlightened." But Jesus said, **"I am the light of the world."** Other religious leaders say, **"Follow me and I'll show you many doors that lead to God."** Jesus said, **"I am the door."** Quite a difference? If there were to be a sign on the top of the narrow door, it would not read Hinduism, Buddhism, Islam, Universalism, or even any Christian denomination. It would simply say Christ Jesus.

For a long time, people tried to harmonize the various religions of the world. But there are drastic and irreconcilable differences between Christianity and all other belief systems. Every other religion is based on people doing things through their struggling and through their striving to earn the good favor of God. They say people have to use a Tibetan prayer wheel or they have to go on pilgrimages. When I was in India and cruising down the sacred (but garbage strewn) Ganges River, I saw multitudes of Hindu pilgrims washing themselves in the River for spiritual cleansing in order to receive favor with one of their gods. Or, other religions claim followers have to give alms to the poor, or they have to avoid eating certain foods, or they have to be circumcised, or they have to perform a certain number of unspecified good deeds. One day when I was walking a local shopping mall, a lady came up to me and asked if she could do anything for me. Nothing wrong with that, but she stated she must do three required good deeds a day, perhaps as some sort of penance. Some have to pray in a certain way, or they have to go through a cycle of reincarnation. They are all attempts to reach out to God.

But, in terms of saving grace, Jesus Christ is God reaching out to us—not we to Him. Jesus taught the opposite of what those other faiths teach. He said that nobody could do anything to merit heaven, so you might as well stop trying. He said that we're all guilty of wrongdoing. That's consistent with human nature, isn't it? That's consistent with our experience. We know that not a single person today could rightfully claim to be perfect. Jesus also said that our wrongdoing separates us from our God because God is holy and perfect. Again, that's consistent with our experience, isn't it? Haven't you had times in your life when you've felt distant and disconnected from God? I know I have. Our rebellion, our wrongdoing, our sin separates us from God because He is perfect and He is pure, and He is holy. Because God is a righteous judge who by his very nature must judge wrongdoing, our wrongdoing has to be paid for.

Because he loves us, because Jesus and God the Father are for us and not against us, Jesus voluntarily offered himself as our substitute to pay the penalty that we owe because of our wrongdoing. When we receive his sacrifice on our behalf, we become reunited with God forever; because Jesus Christ did what needed to be done on the cross. We just need to receive him by faith.

There are other fundamental differences. For instance, Christianity claims that there is one eternal God who created the universe. But Hinduism claims everything is God. Islam denies that Jesus was God. All of these beliefs cannot be true at the same time; they contradict each other too severely. All religions are not the same. While other religious leaders can offer wise sayings and helpful advice and insights, only Jesus Christ, the perfect Son of God, is qualified to offer himself as payment for our wrongdoing. No other religious leader even pretended to be able to do that. Theologian R.C. Sproul puts it this way: "Moses could mediate on the Law. Mohammed could brandish a sword. Buddha could give personal counsel. Confucius could offer wise sayings. But none of these men was qualified to offer atonement for the sins of the world." Jesus alone was qualified.

The second myth about religion is that although different, Christianity is one philosophy among many. This second myth is related to the first myth. They interplay with each other. They overlap a bit. The second myth says that even though Christianity might be different, it's just one philosophy among many, and it's only as valid as any other religion. In other words, even if there are differences between religions, they all have equal claims on the truth. This is the idea that you have your truth, and I have my truth. This is the postmodern claim of academic secular humanists so prevalent in our current culture. This myth is appealing because on the surface it seems to reflect the pluralistic attitude we have in the United States.

Differing attitudes are good. The Bible tells us that those of us who are followers of Jesus need to be loving, respectful, and accepting toward people of all faiths. Under our Constitution, all religious viewpoints are equally protected. Anybody can believe whatever they want. But the problem is that some people jump to the erroneous conclusion that because different philosophies are equally protected, they must be equally valid. That's just not the case.

The concept behind what our Supreme Court calls the "marketplace of ideas" is that truth and falsehood would grapple in unhindered debate, so that in the end, truth would prevail. So even though all religions are equally protected under our Constitution, this has nothing to do whatever with whether they are based on truth. Of course, this gives anybody the freedom to make the claim, as Jesus did, that they are the way and the truth and the life; that they are the only way to God. Anyone is free to make that claim. The question is, how do we know that Jesus was telling the truth when He made His claim? Jesus backs up his claim with unique credentials. Jesus authenticated his claim of being God by living a perfect life, by embodying the attributes of God, and by fulfilling dozens and dozens of century-old prophecies, written hundreds of years before He came to this planet that He fulfilled against all mathematical odds. Odds that in effect created a fingerprint that said whoever fit this fingerprint would be the long-awaited Messiah; the Son of God. Throughout history, only Jesus fulfilled those prophecies. Unlike other religious leaders, Jesus also authenticated who he was by performing great miracles in broad daylight, in front of skeptics. He demonstrated his mastery over nature. He demonstrated his mastery over sickness. He demonstrated his mastery over death by bringing Lazarus back to life after four days in a cold, damp tomb. In the most spectacular demonstration of his deity, Jesus fulfilled his own prediction by being resurrected from the dead, in an historical event that was witnessed by more than 500 people and that sparked a spiritual revolution which has been unparalleled in the history of the world. Christianity is not just a philosophy; it is a reality. Jesus didn't just claim that he is the one and only Son of God. He validated his claim with convincing evidence like nobody else in history.

The third myth about religion is that Christians are narrow-minded to think Jesus is the only way to heaven. Now I'd agree that Christians are narrow-minded if there are many roads to God and they are just claiming; "Ours is the best." But that's not what Christians are saying. They are saying that the truth of the matter is that somebody has got to pay the penalty for the obvious wrongdoings that keep us separated from God. By virtue of His sinlessness and by virtue of his divinity, Jesus is the only one qualified to be our substitute. That is the reality of the situation. It is not narrow-minded to act in accordance with the evidence and to pursue truth.

Every person is born with a terminal spiritual illness called "sin." The reason that those of us who follow Jesus cling to him so tightly is that he is the Great Physician who has the only cure. I mean, we could try to scrub away our sins with good deeds, but that will not work. We can sincerely think with all of our hearts that there are other ways of dealing with it. But we would be sincerely wrong.

The truth is that only the Great Physician offers a treatment that will erase the stain of sin. He has credentials and credibility to back him up. So when we turn to Him, we're not being narrow-minded. We are acting rationally, in accordance with where the evidence points. In addition to not being narrow-minded, it is anything but snobbish for Christians to believe that. For a Christian to take an attitude of being holier than thou or better than anybody else is totally contrary to the teachings of Jesus. It's not snobbish to believe that Jesus is the only way.

Let's pretend there are two clubs. The first club only admits people who have earned their membership. In order to get into this club, you have to buy your membership or obtain superior wisdom. You've got to fulfill a long list of demands. You've got to somehow attain certain spiritual advancement. You've got to go through cycles of reincarnation or whatever. Despite their best efforts, people will not make the grade, and in the end, the door will be slammed in their face. They're not going to be good enough. They're not going to make the qualifications to get in. This is what other religions are saying when they teach that people have to try and try to work their way to God. But Christianity is different. Christianity is like the club that says anybody who wants in is invited in because Jesus has already paid for his or her membership. Rich or poor, regardless of your ethnic heritage, regardless of where you live, we would love to include you. Entry is not based on your qualifications. Entry is based only on a person accepting Christ's invitation. It's not just another religion, but rather a relationship with Him as Savior and Lord. That is what Christianity is all about. Which faith system is being snobbish? Christians aren't saying they're better than anybody else. Christianity is unique. It cannot be reconciled with any other religion. Christianity backs up its truth claims with credentials and credibility of Jesus Christ that are not duplicated by any other spiritual leader, and He is the same, yesterday, today, and yes, forever.

Let us keep in mind the magnificent words of hope expressed by Paul to you and me in 1 Corinthians 15 as to Christ's coming and our eternal life with Him.

> **"In the twinkling of an eye, at the last trumpet, for the trumpet will sound, and the dead will rise imperishable, and we the living shall be changed"**(15:52). **"But thanks be to God, who gives us the victory through our Lord Jesus Christ. Therefore, my beloved brethren, be steadfast, immovable, always abounding in the work of the Lord, knowing that your toil is not in vain in the Lord"** (15:57–58).

Let's always cling to the promises of God's Truth for the meaning of life. Let not your heart be sad by all these latter-day events. Be faithful, strong, and steady till the day we are heaven sent.

www.ingramcontent.com/pod-product-compliance
Lightning Source LLC
LaVergne TN
LVHW092054060526
838201LV00047B/1390